My Trip to the Start-Up World

aka Voice of FinTech, Season 1

RUDOLF FALAT

Copyright © 2020 Rudolf Falat
All rights reserved.

Edited and Typeset by Amnet Systems
Cover design by Amnet Systems
Images by Africa Studio and whiteMocca / Shutterstock.com

DEDICATION

To my biggest fans, my parents

CONTENTS

Acknowledgments   vii

1	Introduction	1
2	Key Topics	3
3	Incumbents	6
4	Investors	14
5	Start-Up Founders	23
6	Incubators or Accelerators	40
7	Thought Leaders or Influencers	47
8	Events	63
9	Additional Resources	70
10	Conclusion	85

About the Author   87
References   89

ACKNOWLEDGMENTS

Thank you to F10, FinTech incubator and accelerator in Zurich, specifically Andy Iten and Lisa Schröder for being the first guests of the Voice of FinTech podcast.

Thanks to FinTech News Switzerland for sharing some of the content on its website.

Thanks to dealroom.co for providing research resources.

Thanks to SIX and HITS. The Financial Markets Series of Voice of FinTech podcast were brought to you by SIX, the Swiss Exchange Group, and The InsurTech Series were brought to you by HITS - House of InsurTech Switzerland, a Generali company.

1

INTRODUCTION

When I was deciding what to study in college, I narrowed my choices to finance and law. I was, and I still am, interested in what explains how society runs, and for me, these two disciplines were the key. I ultimately chose finance as it enabled me to move around the world more easily. I worked in finance all my life, from the financial departments of a major blue-chip multinational in New York, Vienna, and Lausanne to investment banking in London and then corporate development in banks in London and Zurich.

I then made a turn toward the start-up world. Why? When I looked back at my twenty-odd-year career in the corporate world, I asked myself when I truly enjoyed it. The answer was obvious: when the business was growing! So I wanted to explore the world where the word "growth" is an imperative from the early morning until, very often, late at night.

I started mentoring start-ups in Zurich, London, and Paris, and I have also invested in some, mainly technology-led ones. I took many cool courses, from the Oxford FinTech course to INSEAD's Innovation in the Age of Disruption and MIT's Digital Transformation, among others.

In June last year, I started a podcast called Voice of FinTech that maps out the Swiss and European FinTech scene. This podcast aims to inspire entrepreneurs to start new ventures. Also, more broadly, it intends to connect FinTech enthusiasts with various key actors and resources in the ecosystem. I approach FinTech in its broadest sense. FinTech to me means almost any start-up or a scale-up that leverages technology and serves or aims to disrupt the financial services.

This book leverages many of my podcast interviews with incumbents partnering up with start-ups, early-stage investors, start-up founders, and start-up incubators or accelerators in Switzerland and thought leaders or influencers, across Europe, and in the United States and Asia. It is meant to connect the dots and share what I have learned through interviewing my podcast guests and conducting related research.

Enjoy!
Rudolf Falat

2
KEY TOPICS

FinTech. So what is it really?

A few years back, I thought FinTech equals some payment app or a P2P lending platform and that's it. If you read this book or if you listened to the Voice of FinTech podcast, you probably realized that is not the case. You see, to me, FinTech can be almost any start-up or a scale-up business except for a life sciences start-up. I talked to start-up or scale-up founders whose companies mainly have a tech angle but also deal with financial services. We also talked about digital platforms for trading art in a live event. Any platform or technology where consumers trade or exchange items of value or look for ways to spend their money, save, or invest can be called a FinTech.

InsurTech is a slightly different animal but not by much. Many of us associate dealing with an insurer with a visit to a dentist. Well, it doesn't have to be that way. There are many technologies that insurers can use not only to save costs but perhaps surprise and delight their customers—unless, of course, they can develop such technologies or solutions themselves.

In the podcast, we also cover RegTech. Post-financial crisis of 2007–8, many banks invested heavily in their compliance functions. That doesn't mean that a compliance job is a job for life, as in the good old days. It also doesn't mean it's a stress-free, nine-to-five kind of experience. So where is the opportunity for start-ups? Digitizing and automating processes so that humans can free up more time to think and exercise judgment.

Blockchain is a word that divides many, from the anarchists to the conservatives, from crypto to a blockchain that will sort out every problem on the planet—or not. In this book and the podcast, we focus on reputable leaders in the blockchain world who see the benefits of decentralized solutions but also the need to accommodate the requirements of highly regulated financial services.

Artificial intelligence. It seems that AI has replaced blockchain as the buzz word of the year (until a certain virus wiped it off web traffic too). Similarly, as in the blockchain world, many start-ups that introduced themselves to an AI company and were nowhere near using AI have quietly toned down the AI messaging. What we are really dealing with here is machine learning. However, given the rise of the processing power and large amounts of data, there is hope that AI will improve and free humans of dull, repetitive tasks and let them what they do best—and that is to create.

Sustainability is another buzz word, however, thankfully, one that is becoming a mainstream theme for investors. In the podcast, we talk to several guests about how to enable investors to choose their portfolios in line with their values, in addition to the financial goals or education and partnerships on the topic to make sure the financial world takes these matters seriously and, more importantly, sincerely.

We also cover WealthTech in the podcast as wealth management and private banking are so essential to Switzerland. Are Swiss banks early adopters of innovative technologies? After focusing their efforts on pushing private bankers to bring in more assets, increasing lending, and cutting costs, how can they go further? There are many fabulous solutions out there to make private bankers "smarter" and more productive when looking after their clients, and I had a great opportunity to talk with some of them on the podcast.

With technology overall, there should be synergies between tech and FinTech and among Big Tech B2C, Big Tech B2B, and banks. That's where firms like IBM or SAP come in, and we share some of their work as it relates to financial services or FinTech.

Entrepreneurship: can you learn it? Yes? No? Maybe? I believe there is no substitute for doing, especially when it comes to starting one's business. However, with the odds of succeeding as slim as they are, why not turn to others and learn from them? That's the ultimate reason for the Voice of FinTech podcast, its book tips, course recommendations, and live events.

3

INCUMBENTS

Many of you have heard of the innovation theater. It's not a myth or a complaint by someone who pitched to a big corporation and got rejected. It's often true. However, when you read the late Professor Clayton Christensen's classic, *The Innovators Dilemma*, you may appreciate that ignoring disruptive innovation within the value systems of large incumbents and the incentives of their managers may make sense. For a particular set of values and customers, it may not be worthwhile to spend huge amounts of money and effort on a disruptive innovation that may or may not work out—and who knows when—especially when managers deciding about allocation of resources may not be around then.

That said, I still believe that the growth should always remain an imperative, even for a 150-plus-year-old institution. That institution may have grown from a tiny start-up, one-person shop in a garage to tens of thousands of employees. It may have so many layers of management that many of them are detached from producing value in the front office. Instead, they may accrue a great deal of value from engaging in corporate politics. There is a way to optimize this and have a large company where people are still able to see the final goal: serving customers in a way that provides added value, thinking about the long term, and coming up with new and innovative ways of serving customers in better and better ways, which should lead to the growth of both the topline and bottom line.

Whether you encounter a large corporation that hasn't realized it yet or if you are lucky and dealing with one that has, when it comes to the innovation and corporate ventures teams, you have to engage with true believers in innovation and not actors. I've tried my best to find such believers for my podcast, and here they are:

AXAnauten—Open Innovation with AXA

In an interview with Claudia Bienentreu, head of Open Innovation AXA Switzerland, also known as AXAnauten, she explained why and how AXA partners up with start-ups.

Claudia also talked about the benefits of cooperation with start-ups, both for incumbents and start-ups. She appreciates that they are much bolder and faster. However, while AXA can benefit from working with them, start-ups can also benefit from working with an incumbent like AXA. Claudia feels that partnering with start-ups is surely the right way to do innovation nowadays. For example, AXA is very proud of its cooperation with Veezoo, a data science start-up. Veezoo helps AXA analyze and visualize sales data. In turn, AXA is rolling out Veezoo's tool to agents, who love the program, thanks to which they have a better view of their sales and client interactions. That's a tool that AXA did not develop itself.

We also talked about what founders should watch out for when they seek to cooperate with incumbents. Claudia explained it's crucial that when start-ups approach AXA, they know what they're doing. In other words, they have the first product in the market and already have the first clients. Then AXA is happy to see how such start-ups might fit into its business and how they might solve a problem that the clients have. It's always a question of the right timing, of course. The team fit is essential: start-ups have to be able to work with corporations, which is sometimes not easy.

IBM Innovation Ecosystem—Start-Up with IBM

In an interview with Pascal Allot, IBM innovation ecosystem director, he related how IBM offers credits to start-ups using its software such as IBM Watson, offers Design Thinking workshops, and organizes data sciences and other related meet-ups. We talked about what IBM offers start-ups in Switzerland to support them on their journey. We also discussed Big Tech's interest in financial services and most likely areas of innovation focus related to FinTech.

Pascal described his team's mandate to promote innovation within IBM Switzerland and the innovation with its customers, especially the start-ups. For example, IBM provides the following resources or organizes activities:

- IBM runs a Design Thinking workshop for start-ups, wherein it brings start-ups to the IBM studio.
- IBM also provides credits to start-ups to use IBM technology. This can be up to US$120k per year, so it's a huge investment.
- Also, start-ups can get support from IBM to develop their MVP and to make use of introductions to IBM's traditional enterprise clients, which is especially relevant for B2B start-ups.
- IBM organizes various meet-ups, such as those related to data sciences, at the IBM Garage.

Innovation at Generali

In an interview with Anne-Katrin Maser, leader of partnerships and ecosystems at Generali Switzerland, we talked about why open innovation is key for Generali and how Generali cooperates with start-ups through its innovation garage, partnerships, or participation in the F10 incubator/accelerator.

Among other topics, I asked Anne-Katrin how close or far start-ups' ideas must be for it to make sense for Generali to partner with them. Anne-Katrin explained that Generali takes a fairly broad approach to dealing with start-ups. If there is some nexus with Generali's business, that definitely works, which is excellent because otherwise the ecosystem approach or open innovation would hardly succeed.

We also covered examples of start-ups that cooperate with Generali, such as:

- Billte digitizes and automates the entire invoicing process to simplify the invoice process for Generali customers (built together with Generali).
- Imburse provides hassle-free integration into the global payments ecosystem.
- Shift Cryptosecurity offers a hardware wallet for private keys.
- Creditgate24 is a P2P loan platform that connects borrowers with investors with insurance in case the borrower dies so the debt doesn't pass on to an heir.
- Klara is a digital assistant for helping SMEs, managing payments, and bookkeeping.

Soph.IA Summit—Innovation and Start-Ups in the French Riviera

We caught up with Etienne Delhaye, executive director of Sophia Club Enterprises and organizer of Soph.IA Summit, and Michele

Bezzi, research manager at SAP Security Research in Sophia Antipolis, during the Soph.IA Summit to learn more about Sophia Antipolis and SAP AI-related research.

Etienne explained the origins of Sophia Antipolis, a fifty-year-old complex on the French Riviera, near Nice. Many companies have their R&D hubs there; at first, they were mostly telecom companies, but now perhaps the biggest focus is artificial intelligence. Sophia Club Enterprises is the leading club of entrepreneurs on the French Riviera. Such clubs connect the outstanding engineering university talent in the region with corporations and entrepreneurs.

Michele described how SAP leverages artificial intelligence to combine the power of open-source coding even when working on security software. I quizzed him about how they manage potential vulnerabilities in the open-source code. The answer is having the AI—or, more precisely, machine learning and natural language processing—applied to the code instead of the language. Their tool can be found on Github.

Avaloq.one—A New Marketplace for B2B FinTechs

We talked to Anders Christensen, head of ecosystems at Avaloq. one, about the origins of Avaloq as a FinTech start-up, now providing software solutions to the banks worldwide, and Avaloq's efforts to foster innovation ecosystems through its Avaloq.one platform, enabling B2B FinTechs easier access to Avaloq's banking clients.

Anders explained how the Avaloq founders started selling their banking software to banks in Switzerland literally from the trunk of their car. Today, Avaloq is a large, multinational company serving banking clients worldwide. Avaloq management decided to step up its efforts to work with start-ups when it founded Avaloq.

one. Avaloq.one is essentially a marketplace for B2B FinTechs to leverage Avaloq's banking relationships, using its APIs to avoid integration headaches in return for a share of the revenue. They use a self-sign-up approach and streamlined onboarding specifically designed for start-ups, as opposed to traditional vendor onboarding.

The Financial Markets Series: Open Banking in Switzerland

In an interview with Sven Siat, Head Connectivity at SIX, we discussed the state of open banking in Switzerland; comparison to the state of open banking in the EU and Switzerland; attempts to standardize connectivity between banks and FinTechs (third-party providers) and SIX-developed b.Link platform connecting FinTechs and banks and its user benefits, key clients, and onboarding. What's in store for the connectivity efforts in Switzerland later this year?

More specifically, we covered:

- The state of open banking in Switzerland and comparison to the EU.
- PSD2 in the EU—is it fostering cooperation between banks and FinTechs in a balanced way, or not?
- Can we have one standard worldwide for connecting FinTechs and banks, or will we end up with the electrical sockets situation?
- How does one develop an enterprise-grade platform in Switzerland with multiple stakeholders? Example: pilot data exchange program involving UBS, Credit Suisse, Klara, and Abacus.
- b.Link, a platform for standardized interfaces open to the banks, FinTechs, and software providers, developed

by SIX, enabling them to provide account information or payment services: key clients and onboarding on b.Link.
- What's in store regarding the connectivity of the financial institutions in Switzerland for later this year.

In Switzerland, we are in the early days of open banking and we have several players and initiatives, many focus on technical aspects only. Our approach is a bit different, we not only focus on the technical aspects (we do have the technical expertise to run reliable and scalable financial infrastructure), but I think we also understand the challenges that banks have with regard to legal and compliance matters.

Sven Siat

This episode of the Financial Markets Series was brought to you by SIX, the Swiss Exchange Group.

Open Innovation in Central Europe with VISA
In this episode, we spoke to Ute Koenig-Stemmler, Head of Business Development & Sales Non-Traditional Financial Institutions, Central Europe at VISA about VISA's activities in the region that comprises Germany, Austria, Switzerland, and the Netherlands.

We covered the following topics:

- Ute's Business Development Central Europe mandate.
- VISA's activities in the region and in Switzerland in particular.
- VISA's investment in the FinTech space (e.g., acquisition of Earthport, a cross-border payments services provider or

investment in SolarisBank, Banking-as-a-Platform start-up from Germany).
- VISA's outreach to the FinTech community through VISA Everywhere initiative and their cooperation with Tomorrow, a sustainability-focused bank and Penta, credit cards company for SMEs.
- Views on partnerships with start-ups and VISA's focus on working with companies looking to scale-up, leveraging their network.
- VISA in Switzerland cooperates with Yapeal, first independent Zurich start-up with the FinTech license.

What if money becomes fully electronic, so it would become nothing but electrons and photons moving around the world at the speed of light?

Dee Hock, founder of VISA

4

INVESTORS

I have spoken to some fantastic investors on and off the podcast and through my work in banking over the years. As an LP in a venture fund, you, of course, don't know for many years how fantastic or not they are!

So how do you assess the first- or second-time fund's performance? I think you have two options. First, a common one is to assess the track record of the individuals behind the fund. Second, I believe, is to look at their process. How do they source deals? How do they evaluate them? How do they work with their portfolio companies? Alternatively, both options can be used in conjunction.

This is also relevant for a well-established fund. As you might remember from all the investment products' warnings, past performance does not guarantee future performance. This is especially true in early-stage investing.

These were the key themes we tried to tackle in many of the podcasts with investors. One of the questions that came up more often than not was about sourcing through warm introductions or more widely. While I see the value in this, in leveraging one's network of course, I wish that some of the investors would perhaps leverage technology like AI more to search for the best ideas, wherever they come from, and then use their network to get a reference rather than source ideas solely through the people they already know. Give the best idea a chance!

But more about that in some of the upcoming podcasts.

Odysseus Partners—Venture Builder
Minh Q. Tran, managing partner of InsurTech at Odysseus Partners and former GP of AXA Ventures, based in Paris, talked about why he founded a venture-builder company after many years as a VC partner and explained how it differs from a traditional VC fund.

Minh explained that Odysseus looks for start-ups with reasonable strong growth, not hyper-growth. Then Odysseus intends to help these businesses to build their markets. Minh stated that it's like investing in Uber, on the one hand, and, on the other hand, buying a taxi company to bring customers to Uber. Or it's like investing in Airbnb, on the one hand, and, on the other hand, investing in a real estate company to buy apartments that will use Airbnb to find customers. That's the Odysseus model. This is needed in the world, where funds have too much dry powder, and the start-ups can choose who they want to work with. They are looking for someone who can give them an edge, in addition to money and a great valuation. We also talked about Odysseus' automated web crawler that helps Minh to look for new investment opportunities.

Investiere—Investment Platform for Start-Ups in Switzerland
Investiere is a Zurich-based investment platform for qualified investors to invest in start-ups. In an interview with David Sidler,

head of investor relations at Investiere, he explained how Investiere finds suitable investment opportunities, what investors can expect from the platform, and what start-ups need to do to get on the platform.

I asked David what he would advise founders approaching Investiere to raise funding. Not surprisingly, his key piece of advice for the founders is to do as much as they can on their own before trying to get money from investors. David stressed that the more founders have on the table, the stronger their negotiation position is, and so they should bootstrap for as long as possible. Obvious, no? Well, not to everyone. For example, there's also a lot of money to be gained from the awards and grants, but at the end of the day, while it's essential to have a good pitch, endlessly perfecting a three-minute elevator pitch instead of finalizing one's business model and getting going will be a waste of time.

Redalpine—European Technology and Health Tech VC
I had an interview with Harald Nieder, partner at Redalpine, a European, Zurich-based VC that invests in technology (including FinTech) and health tech businesses in Europe. Harald explained how he started investing in start-ups and what VC firms like his are looking for when doing so.

Similar to the interview with Investiere, we talked with Harald about what the founders should focus on when raising money from the VC. Harald pointed out that while having a beautiful deck is important, being able to present the business case verbally is even more crucial. He explained that if you want to sell a company or an idea, the ability to present orally is an incredibly important point in that process. In fact, he believes that many people probably put too much emphasis on the deck and less so on verbal communication. Founders, remember: you have to sell your company all the time—not only to investors and clients but also to employees. Writing a deck is not enough.

It is also essential for start-ups to remember that when they look for funding, it is very much a two-way process. It's not about just a VC choosing a company to invest in. Start-ups should put a lot of effort into researching who is a suitable funding partner for them. It's essential to look at the companies that a particular VC has invested in and get in touch with them to get an idea about what it is like to work with a specific VC.

Veridian Ventures—Business Angel Syndicate
Marwan El-Hakim, a partner at London-based Veridian Ventures and INSEAD alumnus, spoke about how he started angel investing and how business angel syndicates like Veridian Ventures work.

We talked about the biggest mistakes business angels see when reviewing investment proposals from the founders. Marwan shared his experience that the biggest pitfall is an unreasonable valuation: "I always warn the founders that even if you can get away with an unreasonably high valuation early on, it will come and bite you later on in the future raising rounds."

It's imperative to get that right, and it's always better to ensure long-term success than make a quick buck. The expectation is that there are going to be several rounds of funding. It is crucial to tee up the company for the next one and not to increase the valuation so much that the next funding round may be a flat one or a down one.

We also touched upon where we are in the cycle now (note: it was the summer of 2019). Marwan believes that, on average, we are still at the place in the cycle where there are a lot of companies that are investable, but there's a wide range. There are also many companies that have unreasonable valuations. At the same time, there are also many companies with reasonable ones, and Veridian always engages with them if it believes that the business plan is a good one.

Union Park Ventures—From a Banker to a VC Investor

An interview was conducted with Jatin Rajput, partner at New York-based Union Park Ventures, about his transition from banking to VC investing and his views on technology trends impacting financial services and the global economy as a whole.

We talked about emerging technologies like blockchain, AI and IoT, and 5G and how they will make the storage and transmission of data and value much faster and cheaper. In Jatin's view, that will enable a lot of P2P interaction, which will, in turn, disintermediate much of the intermediation infrastructure that has been built over the years. This trend is effectively the heart of the thesis of Jatin's fund. Jatin and his partners are looking at the following broad themes within this thesis:

- Bridging technology and solutions, which will enable the move from the way the economic model structure is today toward a more data-centric decentralized set-up.
- Digital assets and decentralized applications, which will effectively be built on that infrastructure.
- Embedded finance, which is the transaction layer embedded within the user experience.

Singularity Group—Investing in Exponential Progress and Innovation

In an interview with Evelyne Pflugi, co-founder and managing partner at Singularity Group in Zurich, Switzerland, we talked about what exponential technologies are, Singularity Group's relationship to Singularity University, and how to make money from exponential technologies and innovation today.

Evelyne first defined exponential technologies as the kind that change the world because they are adopted much faster than other technologies, and they grow exponentially. We also zoomed in on how you make money out of these sorts of technologies today. Evelyne explained that the financial or investment industry struggles with identifying where these exponential technologies might end up, what the business models around them will be, and how they create value. However, she outlined how you can better target investment opportunities in this space using the research, know-how, and investment approach that her team put together. Check out the podcast for more.

Soundbite with Eric Sarasin, Chairman of Singularity Group

At the Exponential Finance Summit that took place in Zurich on November 14–15, we spoke to Eric Sarasin, chairman of the Singularity Group and former CEO of Bank J. Safra Sarasin, about the Singularity theme and the start-up scene in Switzerland and Europe.

The main message from our chat was that the incumbent/start-up cooperation, or partnership between the senior business people and young founders, is hugely beneficial for both. This especially holds true in FinTech as it operates in or very near the highly regulated industry of financial services.

Swiss FinTech Investor Day: SICTIC, Unconventional Ventures, and eQTiq

On Swiss FinTech Investor Day, we spoke with Thomas Duebendorfer, president of SICTIC, an early Google employee in Switzerland, about SICTIC's mission, activities, and events like these. SICTIC is one of the best-established and most respected business angel clubs in Switzerland. It started with, and still has, a mainly tech focus, but that now includes FinTech too. SICTIC events include an educational element, start-up pitches, and networking of investors with founders looking to raise funds.

We also talked to Theo Lau, founder of Unconventional Ventures from Washington, DC, in the United States, about how to make banking better for underrepresented groups. Theo is a podcaster, too, and is very active on social media. Her main message to everyone is to leverage new technologies like AI to improve the lives of groups that are less fortunate by increasing their access to the benefits and joys that others take for granted. Inclusiveness is the key!

Lastly, we spoke to co-founder of eQTiq Justyna Rydzewska about its mission to get rid of paper receipts. Justyna and her team are working on a paperless solution for receipts—in the country that loves cash. eQTiq offers a unique API that works with all kinds of merchants' POS systems and allows users to keep electronic equivalents of the receipts in the app on their phone. These can be easily organized and retrieved when filing that warranty claim or backing up your tax deductions.

Terra Ventures—A Sneak Peek into an Israeli VC Mindset

We caught up with Astorre Modena, general partner at Terra Venture Partners, Israel, during the Start-up Funding—VC Talks event in Zurich, organized by FinTech Connector.

Asterro explained the Terra Venture Partners investment approach, the Israeli government's support of innovation, his views on the art of start-up valuation and fundraising, and Israeli-Swiss VC and start-up connectivity. Terra Ventures works closely with the Israeli government, essentially sourcing and executing the deals, and the government very generously funds a larger part of the deal.

Financial Markets Technology—VC Perspective
We talked to Mark Beeston, founder and managing partner of Illuminate Financial, a London-headquartered VC firm with a global mandate, about its investment approach, success stories, and views on the Capital Markets FinTech, as well as WealthTech scene in Europe and globally.

Mark explained that when his fund is thinking about whether to invest in a start-up or not, it does not focus on the tech but rather on a business solution. Is this company solving a real problem? Is the solution fit for a problem it is trying to solve? It's a solution-first and technology-second mindset. It's no use to fall in love with technology that is not relevant for the business.

Investing in Enterprise Technology and Scaling Up: A Bay Area VC Perspective
In this episode, we spoke with Shruti Van Dyke Gandhi, partner at Array Ventures in California, focused on Enterprise Tech including FinTech about her transition from an engineer to a VC investor, Array's investment philosophy and approach, comparison between the West Coast and New York start-up scene with respect to FinTech and more. Shruti is also an adjunct professor of computer sciences at Columbia University in New York.

We covered the following:

- Back story: About Shruti's transition from an engineer to an investor.
- Array's focus area: Enterprise software. Big issues, problems, and pain points—for which you can raise money

early, even pre-revenue but you need to have relevant prior experience.
- Array's investment philosophy: Investing in founders that sell to global customers. Portfolio companies are US incorporated, but in the times of remote working, they may be all over the globe.
- Deal sourcing: The network is vital if you are looking to back early-stage founders. Ideas from accelerators or advisers could be too late! Chemistry with the founders is more important than paperwork.
- Success stories/exits: Simility (AI/ML fraud prevention) acquired by PayPal or Passage AI (Conversational AI) acquired by ServiceNow.
- Learning: Keep on learning to avoid becoming antiquated.
- Is New York better for you if you are a FinTech?

Shruti's key piece of advice for the founders:

> *There is no playbook for the founder's life that you can learn in school, so you need to stay agile and prepare for the curveballs to come at you, expect it and find a way to tackle them, so you become a big business regardless what comes your way.*

5

START-UP FOUNDERS

First of all, hats off to anyone who dares to start their own business! It's a whole different kind of responsibility, bringing in the revenues day in and day out without waiting at your desk for yet another task from your boss.

I have been trying to uncover the factors that contribute to the success or, at the very least, to a higher survival rate of start-ups. You will recognize certain patterns in the interviews that I explain a bit more here.

First, when you are starting your business, look for co-founders who are different from you in terms of backgrounds and also experience or skills. In a small company, there is no space for yes-men or -women. Diversity is crucial because you are not building a company for yourself but for others. How to better know whether you are on the right track than having some of these people right next to you?

Second, think big. I am not suggesting lying to yourself or investors about having a billion-dollar idea when you don't, but be ambitious. Especially when it comes to FinTech or technology ventures, these should be scalable. If you want to raise money from beyond your friends, family, and fools, you will need to think about conquering the world. Nothing else will work for outside investors—trust me. The survival rate of start-ups anywhere in the world is about 10 percent, if not less. Your investors are seeking to beat the public markets and late-stage private markets, so you need to show them that infamous ten-times growth.

Third, numbers. I have seen plenty of beautiful pitches where concepts like the total addressable market or unit economics were either an afterthought or completely missing. If that's your case, don't be surprised that your pet project is not going anywhere. Of course, start-up economics is different than running a business that has been around for 150 years, but it's not a random process. Learn about unit economics before it teaches you a lesson!

Fourth, not to be a bore, but as a FinTech, in particular, let's pay attention not only to governance issues but regulatory matters, not only today's but potential future scenarios.

Here are some great founders I had the privilege to talk to on the Voice of FinTech podcast:

Apiax—RegTech Founder Story

In this interview, Ralf Huber, the co-founder of Apiax, shared why and how he co-founded Apiax, an award-winning Swiss RegTech company with offices in Zurich, Geneva, London, and Lisbon. Apiax provides digital solutions to master complex regulations in the financial services (e.g., a mutual funds distribution rules engine).

Ralf explained the core of Apiax's value proposition. Apiax takes everything from what Big 4 firms are good at, such as having a global network and having the reputation of really understanding the business and regulation in detail. That's where Apiax collaborates with Big 4: they provide the regulatory knowledge (i.e., the rules themselves), while Apiax builds on what they are not good at, which is technology. It is a huge challenge to keep track of all the ever-changing rules in banking and make them easily accessible to client advisors. That's how Apiax helps its clients: by making the regulatory expertise digitally transferable.

DACH—FinTech Founder Story
An interview was held with Franz Hoerhager, co-founder of the home equity diversification platform called Bambus, active in Germany and Austria. Franz explained why and when taking on more debt can be a good idea. Bambus is also a recent graduate of the F10 Accelerator Program in Zurich.

Franz and his co-founder, Patrick, strongly believe that individuals should be able to optimize their capital structures just as corporations do. In Germany, for example, a large portion of the population lives in residences that are fully paid up, and the real estate they own represents the bulk of their wealth. The Bambus team believes there is a healthy level of debt that any individual balance sheet can sustain. That's why Bambus provides home equity loans for the reallocation of wealth for diversification purposes. Bambus allows its clients to put, say, 20 percent of their apartment's value into a real estate portfolio in a different country or take it and put it into an ETF. The goal is to optimize the capital structure of an individual's balance sheet and better manage the risks/return profile, not to provide consumer loans backed by real estate.

Toquity—Cap Table Solution for Founders and Investors by INSEAD Alumni
We conducted an interview with Mazin Biviji, INSEAD alumnus and co-founder of the Paris-based start-up Toquity, about

simplifying everything to do with equity. Toquity is a dynamic cap table solution that leverages blockchain.

Mazin explained how he and his co-founder came to develop a solution for dynamic cap tables for entrepreneurs and investors. Toquity's solution leverages blockchain technology to help founders, companies, and investors manage cap tables, option plans, shareholder lists, and portfolios. The key features of the tool are that it is paperless, dynamic, and transparent and that it runs on the blockchain. It is especially valuable as the start-ups grow and their cap tables become more and more complicated.

Toquity was part of the INSEAD LaunchPad program at Station F in Paris. It makes sense for them to launch their venture there as France was the first country to allow storing equity records on the blockchain last year.

Monito—Stop Overpaying When Sending Money Abroad

An interview was conducted with Francois Briod, CEO and co-founder of Monito, the comparison website for foreign exchange services, an award-winning start-up based in Lausanne, Switzerland, one of the key start-up hubs in Switzerland together with Zurich.

Francois talked about why he co-founded Monito. As students, Francois and his brother started an NGO in Switzerland helping underprivileged kids in Cameroon. They faced up to 15 percent in fees when they were trying to send the money there from Switzerland. Francois and his brother also saw an opportunity: not to be another money transfer service on the list but to become "the list" and to compare all the various options of how to send money abroad. Today, Monito shows customers the best deal for transferring money abroad on its platform.

Silkpay—AliPay and WeChat Interface for European Merchants

In an interview with Annie Guo, CEO and founder of Silkpay, she talks about her passion for running her own company and how Silkpay connects European merchants and Chinese tourists using AliPay and WeChat Pay so they can pay in Europe just like they do at home.

In the interview, Annie described how she got the idea to start her own business. A few years back, she took a taxi in Beijing and tried to pay the driver in cash at the end of the trip. He turned around and asked her to pay with the phone, just like everyone else. When Annie explained to him that she didn't have a wallet on her phone, he stared at her for a few seconds to understand why she didn't. Annie realized that there is a digital revolution going on in China in terms of payments, and Europe is missing out! That's what inspired her to start Silkpay, a payment interface between European merchant payment systems and Alipay and WeChat Pay phone wallets. Now, many merchants in France and, soon, elsewhere will be able to accept payments from Chinese tourists just as has been commonplace in China for quite some time.

RegPac Revolution and F10 Hackathon Singapore

An interview was held with Mona Zoet, founder of RegPac Revolution, a RegTech ecosystem builder and accelerator based in Singapore and F10 Hackathon Singapore's local partner.

Mona described the state of RegTech and the start-up scene in Singapore and contrasted it with the one in Switzerland/Europe. She explained that the FinTech (and especially RegTech) start-ups in Europe started much earlier than in Singapore. The FinTech "movement"—whether it was called that or not yet back then—accelerated in Europe right after the financial crisis. The FinTech scene in Asia started to develop much later, although especially Singapore has been accelerating its development on numerous fronts in the last few years. This development is driven mostly by the government's ambition to turn Singapore into a preeminent financial services hub and a smart city.

However, at a "working level," cooperation between incumbents and start-ups is still much more commonplace in Switzerland and the rest of Europe than in Singapore. As you may expect, Singapore and Southeast Asia are catching up fast at all levels though.

Enterprise Bot—Founders Story: Customer Service That Works

An interview with Ravina Mutha and Pranay Jain, co-founders of Enterprise Bot, described their (sometimes adventurous) entrepreneurial journey so far.

In this interview, I asked Ravina and Pranay why their bot is better than anyone else's. In other words, what is their unique advantage? Ravina responded, "If I were to answer that question in two words, it would be: it works!"

Ravina explained that people often underestimate how difficult it is to make an enterprise-ready chatbot. Most existing chatbots fail to function correctly. When a user types in a request without having to do multiple clicks (similar to interactive voice response [IVR]) over the phone, chatbots often respond with "I'm sorry. I don't understand. Can you rephrase that?" again and again.

That's why Enterprise Bot focuses on leveraging natural language processing (NLP) technology. Its core focus is to understand how humans ask questions in different languages, for instance, English, German, French, Italian, or Dutch. Their bot is learning continuously by using NLP and then provides the response that makes sense to humans, unlike most other chatbots. It makes good sense to be based in Switzerland, where most services are offered in three or four languages.

Yova—Founder's Story: Make the World a Better Place and Make Money at the Same Time

An interview was held with Tillmann Lang, CEO and co-founder of Yova, a platform for retail clients to invest in line with their values. Yova stands for "your values." With Yova, individual clients can effortlessly make sustainable and socially responsible investments.

At the beginning of the interview, I asked Tillman, "Why did you start Yova?"

Tillmann responded:

> *I've never really been excited about finance, and the reason is that I've always found finance very frustrating. Once I got to a point in my life where I wanted to invest some money, I was quite frustrated with what I found out there. For many reasons, I always found it degrading to talk to a bank where people were unwilling or unable to explain to me what I would invest in, and it all seemed overpriced.*

We also talked about how Yova makes it possible for retail investors to customize their portfolios online, focusing not only on the returns (and risk) but also on the nonfinancial aspects like sustainability, various causes they care about, or even religion.

Futurae Technologies—Founder Story: When a Dog Is Not Enough to Protect Your Assets

An interview was held with Sandra Tobler, co-founder and CEO of Futurae Technologies, a Zurich-based cybersecurity start-up. Futurae provides multifactor authentication tools to corporate clients from the financial services, insurance, and health-care sectors.

In addition to describing the Futurae story, I asked Sandra to compare the start-up scenes in Switzerland and Silicon Valley. She explained that in her view, the technology that gets developed in both ecosystems is comparably innovative. Still, in the Bay Area, founders seem to have a bit less industry knowledge. Therefore, especially in FinTech, businesses are often designed from scratch. Entrepreneurs develop their ventures that fundamentally disrupt the existing business models. On the other hand, in Switzerland, many people have worked in the incumbents, saw the anomalies and things that didn't work, and now they want to address these pieces of the puzzle while staying within the system.

Furthermore, when you think about funding the start-up growth, although there is now a lot more venture capital in Europe than in the past, there is still a much larger appetite for investing in early-stage start-ups in the Bay Area. In Sandra's view, you can even pitch with a PowerPoint deck and raise ten or twenty million dollars for the first round, which is unthinkable in Switzerland. In Switzerland, you need to have market traction, you need to have reference customers, and the product must be working before you could even start discussing fundraising with anyone. Also, ticket sizes are a lot smaller. All in all, building a global player from Switzerland (versus from the United States) is very challenging because of the sheer market power that you can make out of the United States as well.

Loanboox—Founder Story: Making Raising Big-Ticket Debt Painless

In an interview with Stefan Muehlemann, founder and CEO of Loanboox and a serial entrepreneur, he explained why he believes in the power of platforms, why raising debt should not hurt, and how he got started with his latest venture. Loanboox is a leading big-ticket debt capital market platform based in Zurich, Switzerland, and active in Switzerland, Germany, Austria, France, and the Netherlands.

I asked Stefan about the beginnings, from an idea to a prototype to an MVP. He explained his next steps after he had an idea for his platform:

> *Before I founded the company, I started to speak to potential clients. The survey that I did was with about thirty potential borrowers and thirty institutional investors. When I got their feedback that this is something that they would love to see, I then tried to find somebody who would help me build a prototype. I did find one of my co-founders, Dario, who is the CTO today, who at that time worked at a large company. He took a three-week holiday and kind of programmed twenty-three days through on that prototype. We spent many all-nighters here in the office discussing things, and in the end, Dario built a prototype for us, and then we showed it to the clients, and they loved it. It was an MVP, minimum viable product. It was not fancy; it had all kinds of flaws, but the clients were able to give us feedback on it, and then we knew they're willing to pay money for such a thing, and that's really where the business case lies.*

SEBA—A Bank for Digital Assets

An interview conducted with Guido Buehler, CEO and founder of SEBA, a fully licensed Swiss bank based in Zug, Switzerland. SEBA is a universal bank for digital assets (i.e., digital twins of financial or real assets).

SEBA was founded and is led by seasoned executives. Its story proves you don't have to be in your twenties to start up your own company! As the trading and use of crypto assets are becoming more commonplace and are also being adopted by institutional investors, there is a need for banking services in this space. For trading digital (or crypto) assets on a large scale, you need custody services, and you need leverage. This is what you can expect from SEBA, a universal bank for digital assets. On top of that, it is an international bank for trading your digital assets.

Check6Wealth—How to Make Reporting Easy and Exciting Again

We had an interview with Johan Pieter (JP) Verwey, CEO of Check6, based in Amsterdam and London and with offices in Zurich, New York, Dubai, and Breda. Check6 is a well-established FinTech company that provides solutions such as data consolidation for wealth management reporting for high net worth individuals, wealth managers, and banks. The goal is to provide clients with a total overview of their wealth, irrespective of the asset class.

JP explained how experienced family office professionals struggled with the lack of holistic investment reporting and decided to start their own company to address the gap in the offerings from banks.

In particular, JP talked about family offices needing a report for all their assets, liquid or not, across all custodians and banks where they have their money. Co-founders of Check6 developed a solution that is a direct feed to the back ends of over eighty banks, which they are now selling to family offices around the world.

Direct Lending for SMEs in Switzerland

Ghassen Benhadjsalah, CEO and co-founder of Acredius, is already a serial entrepreneur, based in Switzerland. We talked about direct lending (or P2P lending) in general, focusing on the Swiss small- or medium-sized enterprises (SMEs). We dove into why this market is an excellent opportunity for both SMEs needing financing and lenders/investors, how it all works, and Acredius's competitive edge compared to other platforms or banks.

Ghassen also explained the difference between crowdfunding and crowdlending or direct (P2P) lending. Crowdfunding often relates to funding future product development, with a share of the proceeds accruing to investors—if there are any! Crowdlending is about providing a loan where you should get back the principal and interest. It concerns much smaller tickets than perhaps a bank would be interested in. That's why the use of technology is so crucial so that many small-scale investors can be efficiently connected with SMEs.

We also talked about the importance of diversification, Ghassen's team proprietary credit scoring, coverage of the entirety of Switzerland, and strategic partnership helping to manage the risks of start-up intermediaries like Acredius. Check out the company's roster of projects for which they are raising money if you would like to invest in Swiss SMEs.

The Danube Valley: Vacuum Labs Example

In this podcast, we talked to Matej Ftacnik, CXO and co-founder of Vacuum Labs, based in Bratislava, Slovakia. Vacuum Labs is a FinTech-focused software engineering powerhouse with over two hundred employees, based in Slovakia, the Czech Republic, and Hungary, and it is building and taking innovations to the markets around the world. Vacuum Labs is building neobanks for incumbents in Asia, for example. Matej talked about what it takes to build a large business like this in the region, leveraging top engineering talent to provide solutions to innovation teams of large incumbents around the globe. He also explained how to get it all done while he's still in his twenties.

Vacuum Labs develops products and services with modern tech stacks. They also organize regular meet-ups, workshops, hackathons, and conferences about advanced front-end technologies. In addition to that, Matej loves to travel and see the world, enjoy good food and whiskey, spend time with his family, and meet new people, as he said, "with the wildest personal stories."

Founder Story: Who Is the Best Research Analyst? Invisage Has the Answer

How do you assess research analyst performance in the MiFID II world? Harsh Dadhich, COO of UK-based start-up Invisage and member of the F10 incubator/accelerator in Zurich, explained the company's solution in this interview. Are popularity rankings useful at all, or should the returns on your portfolio, constructed based on the analyst's research, drive whose research you should read? How do you find out *ex ante*, though?

Invisage's slogan is "from research complexity to investment clarity," meaning helping investors find out which research is worth paying attention to and also worth paying for. Harsh stressed the importance of research in active asset management. Invisage's solution for the buy-side is essentially a model portfolio approach that improves the predictability of outstanding performance following a given analyst. This approach attempts to beat the analysts' popularity contests online or the award shows in their ability "to see the future."

Swiss FinTech Awards 2020—And the Winners Are . . .

Swiss FinTech Awards is a prestigious awards show with a conference that, due to the pandemic, is planned to take place later in the year. However, we already know the winners, and here is what we covered in the podcast when we talked to them after the award announcement.

In this bonus episode, we were talking to Oliver Bussmann, CEO and founder of Bussmann Advisory and jury member of the Swiss FinTech Awards, about digital transformation in banking, the FinTech start-up community, blockchain, and his views on the finalists this year and the winners of Swiss FinTech Awards 2020. Oliver, also a well-respected FinTech influencer in the German-speaking world, explained his philosophy when advising corporations:

> *There is a generational change of the CEOs, who understand that the industry is going through a massive business model, operational model, and structural change. Somebody who went through strategy and execution changes and is well connected to the FinTech start-up community is very helpful to guide them.*

Further into the podcast, Oliver detailed his advice on digital transformation to private equity investors, activities in the blockchain world, and his perspectives on the award winners as a juror.

We also spoke to Andy Iten, co-founder and member of the board of F10, Switzerland's only FinTech-focused incubator and accelerator. F10 won the FinTech Influencer of the Year award.

We talked about the start of the incubation program in Singapore, an online version of the F10 Hackathon in Zurich this year (which is used to attract and source teams for the next batch of the program for F10), and cooperation with corporate members. Last but not least, we discussed the new Scale-Up Program in Zurich. Check out the F10's website for more.

Daniel Sandmeier, CEO of Instimatch Global, explained how his digital platform brings together institutions that have excess cash deposits or need cash, replacing the traditional voice or chatroom markets. Instimatch won the Growth Stage Start-up of the Year award.

The final interview was with David Bloch, CEO and co-founder of Legartis and a lawyer. David makes life easier for lawyers and corporate clients by taking routine work out of the contract review by leveraging AI and allowing people to focus on more value-added tasks. Legartis is the Early Stage Start-up of the Year award winner.

Founder Story: Last Mile in Data Analytics with Luminant Analytics

In this episode, Renu Ann Joseph, founder and CEO of Luminant Analytics, a Swiss-American InsurTech start-up, talked about the "last mile" when it comes to using data science and data analytics in the insurance industry. What does Renu mean by this? Inside big corporations, it has become fashionable to set up data science teams. More often than not, there are multiple ones working in silos. On top of fragmentation, such data science teams struggle with connecting the dots, providing useful insights, and integrating with existing legacy infrastructure. This is where the InsurTech start-ups like Luminant fill the gaps.

More broadly, we also talked about the undeniable fact that open innovation benefits both insurers and InsurTechs, not just one party or the other. Renu also shared some early thoughts on the impact of COVID-19 on start-ups and the insurance industry. In particular, we dove into the need for empathy in difficult times, balanced with concerns of the insurers over creating a precedent of paying out for damages that were not factored into pricing.

Luminant Analytics participated in the F10 acceleration program in 2018. Today, Renu spends her time between Basel, Switzerland, and Hartford, Connecticut in the United States, taking advantage of proximity to the major international insurance hubs.

Founder Story: Pivoting to Scale with Rapyd and Guest Co-host Adelle Grisaffe from RFi Group's Global Digital Banker Podcast

In this bonus episode, together with Adelle Grisaffe as a guest co-host, we interviewed Sarel Tal, VP EMEA from Rapyd, a London-based FinTech-as-a-service platform. Rapyd provides APIs that help integrate local payments and FinTech capabilities. Adelle is a London-based Australian and the producer and host of Retail Finance Intelligence (RFi) Group's podcast, Global Digital Banker.

With Adelle, we talked to Sarel about pivoting from B2C to B2B to accelerate scaling up, Rapyd's unique advantage over competitors, and the state of open banking in Europe. We also covered short- and long-term threats and opportunities coming of the current health crisis for start-ups and FinTechs in particular. Luckily for Rapyd, they have just raised another successful round of funding and are ready for internal expansion, leveraging their B2B model.

Founder Story: In Vino Veritas—How to Invest in the Wine Businesses

In this episode, we talked to Maxime Debure, INSEAD alumnus, former winemaker, and management consultant, about investing in wine versus investing in wine estates, either through crowdfunding or private equity type of deals. His business, Wine Funding, helps winemakers obtain equity financing to help them grow their businesses in France and around the world.

Wine Funding is headquartered in Bordeaux, France, but Maxime spends an enormous amount of time on the road, scouting opportunities for investors—for example, vineyards in California, South Africa, or Portugal, as you might expect. Maxime's goal is to connect motivated investors with outstanding opportunities and provide winemakers alternative sources of funding that perhaps weren't open to them until recently.

As expected, Maxime is also a fine wine connoisseur and can recommend true gems for wine lovers around the world. He is also an author of several books on the wine business.

Core Banking in the Cloud with Thought Machine
In this episode, we talked to Paul Taylor, CEO and founder of Thought Machine, a London-headquartered cloud-native core banking technology company, about benefits of running core banking infrastructure in the cloud, how the banks' thinking about this has shifted over the last few years, Thought Machine's recent funding round ahead of the further growth phase, and the importance of good coding practices in growing software companies and banks.

Paul explained how he has been involved with computer sciences for decades and how he started and sold his business to Google but ultimately started yet another business, which is Thought Machine.

I quizzed him about banks' attitudes toward using cloud, citing client data concerns. Paul explained that the attitude has recently changed tremendously, and even large banks now appreciate the benefits of running their infrastructure from the cloud. Solutions to client data concerns include splitting the client identifying data so they stay within the bank's jurisdiction and anonymized transaction data stored in the cloud.

We also covered the potential issues of banks' dependency on outsourcing and creating a legacy infrastructure, just this time in the cloud. Paul clarified that while Thought Machine provides modular solutions to banks, the company strives to avoid unnecessary modifications and, by doing so, lets banks benefit from scalability and agility that would not be feasible with traditional approaches. Similarly, standardization provides clarity and transparency so the banks can feel comfortable using outside vendors. Sharing development costs among a number of Thought Machine's customers is the only way to go in any case.

Emerging Technology Due Diligence—How?
Doing due diligence is never an easy exercise. Especially when you want to form a view on emerging technology—is it going to work or not? Are there bugs in the code that are so hard to find they will only manifest themselves when the product will be live and overloaded by interest? Is it purely technical diligence? Is it a conversation or a tour? Or both?

These are some of the topics we covered with Rodney Reis, co-founder and CEO of Avalia Systems, based in Yverdon-les-Bains, close to Lausanne, Switzerland.

6

INCUBATORS OR ACCELERATORS

I am a foreigner who has been fortunate enough to live in Switzerland for more than ten years. I think it's a fantastic country. People abroad think of Switzerland, and immediately skiing, chocolate, watches, and things like that come to mind. Switzerland, however, has a huge start-up scene and, especially in Zurich, a FinTech scene. Lausanne is another huge start-up hub with as many start-ups as Zurich (c. 500) but only one-third of the population! You will meet great engineers coming out of ETH in Zurich or EPFL in Lausanne. They are inventing amazing technology, and innovative spirit is commonplace.

However, I don't see the start-up founders often pairing up with the founders from business schools. And that's where the incubators come in. For example, I have been mentoring at F10, which is also called the Home of FinTech. I believe F10 and others fill in the vacuum in terms of education. We can debate whether you can teach entrepreneurship or not, but I think that surely there are certain things that you could learn as a founder that would improve your chance of survival. This includes learning about what goes into a successful pitch, what business canvas is, how to test user interfaces, and the like.

In my podcast, I talked to a few hubs with different focuses, and they all have one thing in common. They try to improve start-ups' chances of survival through teaching and connecting them with incumbents. Here are the key takeaways.

F10—The Home of FinTech

The first-ever Voice of FinTech podcast episode is an interview with Andy Iten, co-founder of F10—also known as the Home of FinTech—a leading FinTech incubator and accelerator in Switzerland, and Lisa Schroeder, program manager at F10. It aired on June 11, 2019.

Andy explained what F10, a Zurich-based FinTech incubator and accelerator, does. It solves the problems of three different groups of stakeholders. First are the start-ups. They need help to get traction, access to customers, and funding. F10 helps them get there. The second type of stakeholders is the corporate partners, the members of F10. They are looking for innovative ideas and investment opportunities, so F10 gives them a high-quality deal flow as well as opportunities to collaborate with start-ups. Third is the external investors who invest in the start-ups that F10 supports.

In the second segment, Lisa described F10 programs. F10 offers a forty-eight-hour Design Thinking Idea Boot Camp, which aims to turn ideas into validated prototypes. It also provides a six-month prototype-to-product program (P2), wherein early-stage start-ups come to Zurich to work on their prototype, and at the end of the program, they leave with an MVP. There is also a program for the later-stage start-ups, called the P3: Product to Market.

Only twenty-five teams from hundreds of applications get accepted into a program. Moreover, F10 ensures the quality of the participants' work. If a team doesn't hit certain milestones, it has to leave the program.

Founders Factory—Global Partner for Start-Ups and Scale-Ups

An interview was conducted with Kelvin Au, head of venture at Founders Factory in London, about how he got to do what he loves and what Founders Factory, a global technology incubator and accelerator, is all about.

Kelvin talked about Founders Factory's original thesis that there's no reason corporations and start-ups can't coexist. They should and should also mutually benefit each other very much. It's just that in the past, there were not many successful corporate venture business models that would have worked. Honestly, traditional corporates often struggle with innovation. That's why Founders Factory is trying to set up a format or platform so that corporations and start-ups can mutually benefit while building future stars of the industry and hopefully have fun as well. Founders Factory in London has over seventy people who can provide expertise in several verticals and help start-ups maximize their chances to make an impact in the world. (Note: Since then, they have also expanded to Paris and other areas.)

digitalswitzerland—Platform to Drive Digital Transformation across the Country

We interviewed Matthias Zwingli, program manager of start-up enablement at digitalswitzerland. digitalswitzerland is a multistakeholder initiative of over 150 members to strengthen Switzerland's position as a leading innovation hub. It aims to engage the government, businesses, academia, and the public to move Switzerland forward.

Matthias described what digitalswitzerland would like to achieve in the Swiss start-up ecosystem. He explained that while there are incredible start-ups there from a technological perspective, they often lack the speed when trying to grow. Most of the start-ups take ten years to achieve some scale, which is very slow (even though there is a lot of DeepTech and HealthTech in Switzerland, which affects these stats a little bit). Moreover, start-ups in Switzerland often grow only to the SME level with around fifty staff members. That's why Matthias and his team strive to foster the global spirit in Swiss start-ups. They firmly believe that digital businesses are not meant to be built just for eight million people but for the world. I could not agree more.

Soundbite with Geoff Ralston: Y Combinator Visiting Europe

"I see a tremendous spirit of entrepreneurship taking off in Europe," Geoff Ralston, president of Y Combinator, said to me when we met at Station F in Paris.

Geoff explained that great new companies will come from Europe or anywhere on the planet, not just the United States. We caught up during the INSEAD LaunchPad event at Station F in Paris. It was good to hear some encouragement from Geoff, the founder of Rocketmail, the predecessor of Yahoo! Mail. Y Combinator changed its review process last year and went around the world to meet prospective entrepreneurs instead of flying them to California, as it did in the past, on the lookout for the best ideas and the best talent, wherever it comes from—true meritocracy!

F10 Goes to Singapore

After running two hackathons in Singapore, F10 (the Home of FinTech) from Zurich expanded its flagship program to Singapore in 2020.

In November last year, we spoke with Lisa Schroeder, head of start-up program management at F10 FinTech incubator /accelerator, about the application process and the content. The program goes full steam ahead this year, with some parts delivered online due to the ongoing pandemic.

Seedstars World—Emerging Markets Start-Up Ecosystem Builders

We had an interview with Alisee de Tonnac, CEO and co-founder of Seedstars World, based in Geneva, Switzerland. Alisee is a road warrior, entrepreneur, and ecosystem builder focused on emerging markets. She is also widely recognized as a leading supporter of start-ups in Europe and worldwide and, of course, a role model for many entrepreneurs. Seedstars is an incubator, accelerator, and investor in start-ups, active in over eighty-five countries. Seedstars runs ten entrepreneur hubs around the world, EUR 250m+ raised and 12k+ applications to Seedstars World competitions.

Seedstars is essentially a commercial, for-profit incubator, accelerator, and early-stage investor as well as a consulting firm. With Alisee, we talked about Seedstars's philosophy, start-up competitions, and their start-up support from mentoring to funding. In April, Seedstars promptly changed its flagship event to a fully online version and continues to support start-ups, focusing on emerging markets.

Xoogler.co—Start-Up Community of Googlers and Google Alumni

An interview was conducted with Rune Bentien, managing partner EMEA at Xoogler.co in London. Xoogler.co is a global community of current and former Google employees. The Xoogler.co community consists of start-up founders, early team members, angel investors, VCs, and mentors. It acts as an incubator, an accelerator, a business angel, and a mentoring network for Google alumni (Xooglers). Many of their events this year have been promptly changed to online format with an ease that you would expect from techies like Xooglers.

Xoogler.co is independent of Google but very friendly with it, as you might expect. What a great way to work with former employees! You should check out a wide range of their events, from inspirational fireside chats to training or investor days. For investors, Xooglers know the meaning of the path to scale, so if you are looking to write a large check for a truly investable idea, you won't be disappointed.

R3—Enterprise Blockchain Solutions for Corporations and Start-Ups

Yves Guillaume A. Messy is a blockchain architect and ecosystem builder at R3, an enterprise blockchain company behind Corda blockchain software. As an ecosystem builder, the interview is included in this chapter.

We talked to Yves about how R3 started as a bank-owned consortium start-up to develop enterprise-grade blockchain solutions where it mattered most to the banking shareholders (i.e., related to trading to a leading, standard-setting company for enterprise blockchain).

We also discussed what enterprise blockchain means. It includes solutions that work in a highly regulated environment like financial services. It naturally follows that it's a permission-based blockchain, which is scalable and fit for purpose: it has to make sense for a particular use case. Blockchain at R3 is about providing solutions for particular problems, not a blanket technology that may or may not work for every problem in the world. We discussed the suitability of blockchain for enterprise, including privacy, regulation, and scalability aspects. All in all, this means it is Blockchain 3.0—blockchain for business.

Furthermore, we also covered R3's recently announced cooperation with the F10 incubator and accelerator. Furthermore, Yves also outlined R3 growth ambitions for the world and the DACH region—stay tuned. There is a lot more to come from them.

MassChallenge Lausanne: A Million Francs for You?

In this episode, we talked to Matt Lashmar, managing director of MassChallenge, Switzerland.

He explained the origins of MassChallenge, starting from the financial crisis of 2008 in Boston, Massachusetts in the United States, and aiming to help founders get their businesses off the ground. We also talked about how a guy like him, with a long corporate career, got to lead MassChallenge in Lausanne, Switzerland.

We discussed the main benefits of joining MassChallenge, from proximity to top-class corporate partners, a first-rate mentoring program, and generous prizes without MassChallenge asking for an equity stake. The prize money for the current cohort is one million Swiss Francs. We also discussed their success stories, from food to FinTech start-ups, proving they are an industry agnostic program. Their program continues in 2020, leveraging remote working technologies.

7

THOUGHT LEADERS OR INFLUENCERS

I've met many great people who are relevant to the start-up world, entrepreneurship, and cutting-edge technologies or are, plain and simple, very cool people to talk to.

Many of them show up to events, and it's difficult to reach them otherwise. I find truly successful ones who are self-assured, down to earth, and very easy to deal with.

Here are some key points from our discussions.

Soundbite: *The Future Is Asian,* **by Dr. Parag Khanna**
The Future is Asian is an excellent book by a well-known Indian-American economist based in Singapore, Dr. Parag Khanna.

We caught up with Parag at the Asia Society's event in Zurich, where he shared his views about Asianization in front of a sold-out audience. Parag highlighted that the world has already become more Asian than ever, perhaps without Westerners realizing it. The book focuses on the interconnectedness within Asia that ebbed and flowed throughout history to today. Parag is a fantastic speaker, very active on social media, so please check out his latest views and analysis of how the world may change post-pandemic.

Soundbite: SwissCognitive—The Global AI Hub and We Shape Tech

During the Business Innovation Week in Zurich, we quickly caught up with Dalith Steiger-Gablinger, co-founder and managing partner of SwissCognitive—The Global AI Hub, and Melanie Gabriel, board member at We Shape Tech.

We talked with Dalith about what cognitive technology means:

> *When people think about cognitive technologies, mainly they think about robots, devices, and algorithms. When I think about cognitive technologies, I think about the human being—about how cognitive technologies can support us and can augment the human brain.*

Melanie Gabriel outlined We Shape Tech's mission to drive diversity (gender or otherwise) in the technology sector. For example, We Shape Tech runs many events (in person or online) to drive female participation in tech and innovation to a 50/50 female/male ratio. Check out their awesome events on their website.

Swiss Finance Start-ups and Swiss FinTech Fair

In a fantastic interview with Christina Kehl, co-founder and managing director at Swiss Finance Start-ups, we talked about the efforts of the Swiss Finance Start-ups association to foster cooperation with the government and incumbents, as well as their flagship event, Swiss FinTech Fair.

Christina explained how the association engages with leading politicians in Switzerland to get them acquainted with the start-up scene there and provide the best possible conditions for starting and running new businesses in the country.

This is followed by short, one-question segments with participants of the Swiss FinTech Fair: Julia Holzgreve, director of innovation scouting and strategic partnerships at Keen Innovation; Matthias Kribbel, chief product officer at Tradeplus24; and Christina Reuther, regional head Switzerland, Fintechnews.ch and business development Middle East, Fintechnews.ae.

With Julia, we talked about why she is a believer in open innovation and how Keen Innovation is well positioned to succeed there thanks to their setup, run separately from its shareholders' organization. Matthias explained why it makes more sense to cooperate with banks in Switzerland but why Tradeplus24 is trying to disrupt them in Australia. Christina Reuther explained how global and local FinTech news networks work across the globe, from Asia to Switzerland.

TEDx Zurich: The Power of 10
In a short interview with Florian Bucher, TEDx Zurich co-lead, at their flagship TEDx Zurich event, we talked about TEDx activities in Switzerland, the Power of 10 theme, TEDx Salons, and TEDx Women events. Mind you, 2019 was the tenth anniversary of TEDx Zurich.

As you can guess, the Power of 10 is related to the 10x philosophy often preached by start-up gurus but, unfortunately, only achieved by a few. TEDx is locally organized under license from TED and is dedicated to spreading ideas that are worth sharing, coupled with great entertainment, fantastic delivery of carefully curated speakers (and sometimes also guests), and design.

Voice of FinTech Meets Global Tech Box: An Ultimate Podcast and Vlog Crossover

In this podcast, we talked to Cedric Bollag, founder and host of the Start-up Show, by Global Tech Box, about how and why he started his show, his impressions of the Swiss start-up scene, and a comparison to the Israeli one.

Cedric has become a fixture at start-up events in Switzerland over the last few years. He openly shares his experience from a business student, to a start-up scout in Israel, to a well-known vlogger in Switzerland. We acknowledge that founders need to be honest regarding what they want to achieve, whether it's an SME or having a shot at building a unicorn. We also talked about why Israeli founders look to the world when they are looking for growth and how to take inspiration from that if that's what you want to do.

Check out the Start-up Show, by Global Tech Box, on YouTube; you will find this podcast as a vlog there too.

The Future of Money by SIX—Is Cash Dead?

An interview was held with Alexander Verbeck, head of cash ecosystem at SIX Group in Zurich, Switzerland. SIX is a financial service provider that operates in the infrastructure of Switzerland's financial center, including the Swiss Stock Exchange. We talked about the white paper that Alex and his team wrote called "The Future of Money."

Will we give up on cash and go all-digital in the new decade? Alex and his team concluded that the most likely scenario is a hybrid one, with a significant decrease in the usage of cash but still not fully digital. Let's see if the contactless payments and online deliveries during the lockdowns across the world will accelerate the trend, and people will turn against holding and using cash.

We included the links to the full white paper, summaries, and infograms in the resources section. Look out for the fictional character Felix and his journey with (or without?) money in the future.

You Can't Do It Alone: How to Find High-Quality Talent for Your Venture and What to Look For

We talked with William Laitinen, managing director of Exige International, a UK and Swiss executive search firm specializing in recruitment for global financial companies, especially innovation teams, about what to look for in your co-founders and what traits you should focus on when building a successful team.

William outlined what he finds as key elements that will set you, an entrepreneur or a manager, up for success. When building an effective team, starting with co-founders, one should look for the following traits: diversity, assertiveness, integrity, humility, and resilience.

Diversity. When choosing your co-founders, choose people who are different from you, diverse in their cognitive approach or cognitive skills. This brings a tremendous advantage to your company for a very simple reason: you are not building a product or service for yourself but for others. What better way to understand that than surrounding yourself with people who don't look or speak like you?

Assertiveness. I quizzed William about what he means by this. Is this someone pushing, jumping up and down, and yelling to get the most of their team? Apparently, no. It's about someone raising their hand when they see an issue or when they see something wrong or might have a better idea than a boss.

Integrity. This is a little bit easier to reconcile with humility, but I asked William what he means by this because in a lot of firms, people have become a little bit numb to the notion of integrity, having done way too many online compliance training courses and perhaps lacking it in practice. By integrity, William means honesty, credibility, and trust. It's important to remember that a company effectively is just an imaginary construct. What a company really is a group of people working in a community toward a shared objective, and what communities are built on is trust. You can only work effectively with people when you trust them.

Humility. One of the common misconceptions about humility is that it means you lack ambition. William added:

> *I don't think that's the case. I think humility is an ability to put yourself second. It is a great quality in a leader. Let me give you an example. Let's take a massive figure, someone like Gandhi. Nobody would say about Gandhi that his ambitions were small. He had huge ambitions for the people of India against massive institutional structures, and he did it with peace, but he was also humble. You can, at the same time, have huge ambition. It's just almost this recognition that the company or the mission is more important than you.*

Resilience. I asked William, "Do you have people running around the track, and if they don't give up within the first three hours, it's good; otherwise, they're out? Or how does that work?" William responded:

> *Well, I've just added that to my interview routine now, sir, thank you for that advice. That's what I'm going to use, but how we've been doing it more traditionally? Resilience is one's ability to remain motivated, to act right in the face of change or adversity. I look to see what feeds the motivational*

fire even when it's raining. That's how we see that the person is motivated to get the job done.

Somebody Stole My Unicorn: Make Sure It Doesn't Happen to You
We talked to Christian Meisser, CEO of LEXR, about how to set up your venture from the get-go to minimize potential legal troubles and keep your hard-earned unicorn for yourself.

LEXR is an innovative legal services firm based in Zurich, Switzerland, providing legal services and products to start-ups, especially FinTechs. They focus on technology, FinTech, and digital businesses.

In this podcast, we cover:

- Company: the incorporation of the company (when?)
- IP: intellectual property rights
- Governance: investor, employee, and board relationships
- Endgame: fundraising and exit (or bankruptcy)

And we cover this all in the most pragmatic, to-the-point manner you can imagine for a lawyer. This podcast, of course, does not constitute legal advice, but it is a summary of the high-impact topics you should think through.

When to incorporate your business? One of the key considerations is liability. Of course, you want to protect yourself against potential claims. Or you may think that having an ltd. or a joint-stock company means that you have a business. Well, the truth is that you don't. You start to have a business when you have paying customers. Therefore, when you are starting out, why don't you just have a website to test customer feedback and traction rather than spend time with lawyers setting up a company that may have nothing to do in the end?

IP rights. Once you incorporate and later on, when you will be raising money, investors will want to see that all the intellectual property rights are assigned to the company. So be careful. Don't work on anything using some other company's computer in your day job.

Governance. The board is ultimately responsible for the company. Don't think that if you are a founder and a CEO in one, you cannot get fired. Choose your board wisely, learn about their motivations, and how they work when things go badly. A good idea is to talk to other founders backed up by the same investors you are talking to. How is it to work with them?

Endgame. Nowadays, companies stay private for much longer than they used to. IPOs may also be shelved for later as long as the markets are so choppy. Most likely, you will be looking at a trade sale or a sale to a financial investor. Think about the timing and, if your involvement after a sale is required, about the terms of your continued involvement with the company. Bankruptcy—well, that is linked to the governance point; the board is ultimately responsible and will decide when to file for one, so work with your board to arrive at the best possible result for all.

Listen to the podcast for more examples and color.

INSEAD in Davos

In this bonus episode, we caught up with Peter Zemsky, deputy dean of INSEAD and dean of innovation, after the INSEAD-hosted panel on artificial intelligence (Balancing AI Productivity and Responsibility) in the STG tent in Davos during WEF 2020.

We talked about why INSEAD joined Davos and how the Hoffmann Global Institute for Business and Society needs to participate in conversations with senior global leaders about what it means to lead a business today. Following up on that, we discussed INSEAD's recent partnerships in innovation with Microsoft, Singularity University, and INSEADxBlockchain and INSEAD's investment in a new hub in San Francisco that opened in February 2020.

Paris FinTech Forum 2020

Paris FinTech Forum 2020 took place in January 2020. It was a great way to connect with FinTech leaders from over seventy countries, over 250 CEOs, 170 FinTechs, and more than 2,600 attendees who gathered in Palais Brogniart in Paris.

We talked to:

- Clara Durodie, chair of Cognitive Finance Group, based in London, about the implications of artificial intelligence for financial services (especially wealth management) and about her book, in which she gives advice to boards about how to properly leverage the power of new technologies like AI in their work.
- Ian O'Sullivan, European lead of MasterCard StartPath, based in Dublin, who explained how Mastercard works with start-ups, helping them to get to market and gain scale, providing services to Mastercard customers, and Mastercard's support of female entrepreneurship.
- Susanne Chishti, CEO of FinTech Circle and FinTech Circle Institute, from London, described FinTech Circle's business angel investing, education, and digital transformation acceleration programs, including several FinTech-related books they published, such as a PayTech one that came out this year.

- Emmalyn Shaw, managing partner from Flourish Ventures, San Francisco, who spoke about global scalability and financial inclusiveness. Key message: the only ideas that are investable for VCs are those where there is a clear path to scale.

Finovate Berlin
In this episode, we spoke to Greg Palmer, VP at Finovate, based in San Francisco, a leader in FinTech conferences around the world, about the Berlin edition that took place in February.

In addition to being VP at Finovate, Greg is also the host of Finovate podcast, director of FinTech strategy at Informa Connect, and contributor at Banking Technology, based in San Francisco, California.

We discussed Finovate's concept, how it varies across the globe, and its plans for San Francisco, New York, and Asian editions. Finovate prides itself on organizing live demos of start-ups rather than standard pitches or speeches. However, in Asia, their format is more traditional, with keynote speeches as well, since that's what the local audience prefers. We also touched upon the ever-changing plans of event organizers and the postponement of the San Francisco edition due to the current situation around COVID-19. Check out video demos of the start-ups presenting in Berlin, for example, Apiax, a leading Swiss RegTech company, on Finovate's website.

We also spoke to Myles Stephenson, CEO of Modulr, a London-based integrated payment service for businesses, about the Copernican leap in banking, direct connectivity of FinTechs to the Bank of England, and Modulr's growth plans.

Myles is an Oxford University alumnus and a seasoned executive in the Payments Space based in London, UK. You should definitely check out Modulr's developer portal and sandbox on their website.

Wealth Management versus WealthTech
We talked to Christine (Mar) Ciriani about wealth management challenges and where and how WealthTech start-ups could provide solutions for pain points of client advisors servicing high net worth or ultra-high net worth clients.

Christine is CCO of Finantix, a board member at Barclays Switzerland, and an industry partner at Motive Partners. She is a managing partner and advisor with experience in wealth management, technology and FinTech transformation, and private equity.

One of the key topics we dove into is the adoption of WealthTech and what kind of WealthTech makes sense for incumbents. As industry observers and equity analysts know well, large banks and wealth managers have been focusing on increasing the AuM load per relationship managers, increasing the lending ratio versus AuM, and slashing the costs since the last financial crisis. I asked Christine, "Where does the use of technology and WealthTech fit into all of this?"

She explained that a recently conducted survey found that 47 percent of high net worth individuals stated they would like wealth managers to prioritize digital innovation to improve client experience. They believe that the personalized investment advice they are getting now from their wealth managers is generally poor. That means there is a great opportunity to use WealthTech. Going digital is key to being able to engage in servicing clients today.

In particular, WealthTech can play a major role in identifying and delivering personalized, relevant, actionable, timely, individual service to clients. Large banks have a vast product universe, and distilling a product universe to the relevant client, explaining the products, and educating the client accordingly are challenges. That's where digital tools to support relationship managers (client advisors) can make a difference, especially in an increasingly competitive environment.

We also looked back more broadly at how WealthTech started with the digitalization of existing processes and providing clients with basic information. Now, with a combination of available data and the maturity of digital adoption, banks and wealth managers adopt a wide range of tools focusing on client optimization and operational efficiency elements as well. About five years ago, we first saw a focus on remediation and regulation and, therefore, a lot of tools to automate, for example, AML. We have fortunately moved on to being able to automate real engagement and providing the RM a lot more information. They can provide a richer client experience and have a more exciting dialogue with their clients now. This can make a significant difference that ranges from client profiling, where you can enable a lot more data again in terms of better identifying risks, to focusing more on collaboration using digital tools to help clients drill down and get information to self-serve and help them better understand not only the offerings of a bank but also the impact of such offerings on their wealth.

The InsurTech Series: The Government and the Start-Ups, with Andri Silberschmidt

In this episode, we spoke to Andri Silberschmidt, entrepreneur and the youngest member of the Swiss Parliament. Andri is also the co-founder of Kaisin, a poke bowl food start-up in Zurich, and a senior advisor to the family office Marcuard; he also does some great work with charities.

We discussed his entrepreneurial journey, what drew him to politics, his views on Switzerland as a home for start-ups, the Swiss government's measures to help start-ups deal with the COVID-19 pandemic, and his early thoughts on the world after lockdown.

Andri explained how all of his activities came together and what he, as a co-president of the Start-up Committee in the Swiss Parliament, has been doing to help start-ups succeed. We compared the COVID-19 support measures taken in Switzerland to others, and the pros and cons of those as well. We also touched on the vision of the world post-crisis.

Moreover, we talked about the benefits of choosing Switzerland to start a business, such as a strong rule of law, the presence of a strong start-up ecosystem, and also very successful multinational, mature companies. On the other hand, the ease of doing business needs some improvement: it takes too long to start a company compared to some other countries as many of the administration processes are not yet fully digitized.

We also discussed support measures for start-ups during the COVID-19 crisis, which range from "short-time" work to bridge loans and how the federal government works with cantons to tailor such packages, initially intended for SMEs, to also help start-ups. Find out more in the resources section.

This episode of the InsurTech Series was brought to you by HITS—House of InsurTech Switzerland.

The InsurTech Series: Where to Play with Marc Gruber, VP Innovation EPFL, Lausanne
We talked to Marc Gruber, Vice President Innovation at EPFL and professor of entrepreneurship, about innovation, entrepreneurship, implications for FinTech, InsurTech, and incumbents. In their book *Where to Play*, Marc Gruber, together with Sharon Tal, professor of entrepreneurship at Technion, Israel Institute of Technology, address the issue of the need of start-ups to get to the

target market first versus the reality that more than 70 percent of them end up pivoting anyway. How to pick the right arena/domain early on to make pivoting less costly and increase the chances of success? How does entrepreneurship differ in Europe versus the US or Asia? We also talked about implications for InsurTech and FinTech businesses, but also insurers and banks and their innovation projects. The book *Where to Play* is an excellent complement to the Lean Start-up toolkit.

This episode of the InsurTech Series was also brought to you by HITS - House of InsurTech Switzerland.

Discussion with Janine Haendel, CEO of Roger Federer Foundation

We talked to Janine Haendel, CEO of Roger Federation Foundation, about the foundation's origins and its mission, entrepreneurship, increased focus on performance in the NGO sector, leveraging technology and financial innovation when delivering on foundation's goals in Africa.

Janine Haendel is CEO of Roger Federer Foundation. A lawyer, diplomat, and philanthropist. In this podcast, we discussed:

- Origins and mission of Roger Federer Foundation
- Focus on performance in the NGO sector: efficiency and effectiveness
- Difference between charity and philanthropy
- Improving education in Africa: focus on a teacher
- Leveraging technology
- Making an impact on the aid recipient: village banking

> *I believe in the power of people. They might only need some initial empowerment. We know that a good education empowers children by allowing them to take their future into their own*

hands and play an active part in shaping it. And we trust in the best will of parents that they want to ensure the best possible opportunities for their children. For 16 years my Foundation has therefore been committed to enable parents and local communities in providing these children with the opportunity for a good education. We have reached one million children by today.

Roger Federer

One Year Anniversary Special: Breaking Banks with Brett King

Brett King is a speaker, author, founder, podcast host, pilot, gamer and a scuba diver, based in New York, NY. Founder and host of #1 FinTech podcast and radio show, Breaking Banks. He is also Executive Chairman of a challenger bank Moven. We talked about virtual and live events and their outlook in the post-COVID-19 world, Brett's hit podcast and radio show Breaking Banks, sci-fi as an inspiration for a futurist and future scenarios described in his upcoming book, *The Rise of Technosocialism*, and much more!

More specifically, we discussed:

- Virtual events during the lockdown—are they here to stay? Do traditional conferences have a future?
- Breaking banks podcast and radio show—beginnings, regional spin-offs, focus on the content and high profile guest focus (previous guests included Elon Musk, Boris Johnson, or Bill Gates).
- Science-fiction as an inspiration for the future of banking, whether from near or far future sci-fi. Think Start Trek and Motorola mobile phone! Future worlds with money or without?

- His new book, *The Rise of Tehcnosocialism*: what are the possible scenarios for humans as species. Brett argues the technosocialism, which is a highly automated society, with broad prosperity and ubiquitous technology infrastructure, and provides for health, education and transport is the preferred scenario for humans.
- We talked about how he founded the first mobile bank Moven, and why the team decided to pivot from direct to consumer to enterprise clients. It seems that they were too early and could not get the funding to reach the millions of consumers that VCs wanted to solve by themselves first. Today, Brett and his team believe that way they will have a bigger impact and scale more quickly and get their solutions to 100 million+ customers than say, 10 million which a successful challenger bank could achieve.
- Brett's plans for the rest of the year, including hopefully spending more time in Thailand where he spent a lot of time growing up and resuming speaking engagements from October if the pandemic situation allows.
- How to get noticed - tips for when approaching time-poor influencers like Brett. Be specific in you ask!

Basic bank account should be something that's helpful to the customers, not a passive thing that stores value and charges you interest on your credit card. Secondly, let's raise our total social consciousness and awareness so we understand that things like climate change disruption on society is a choice, it's not inevitable and we can change the future, if we just set our mind to it and get to work.

Brett King

8

EVENTS

I love meeting new people. It's, therefore, no surprise that I enjoy going to meet-ups, conferences, and live events of any kind around the world—while it was safe, of course.

Some people tell me that many of the FinTech conferences lack good content, are too big, or are way too much hassle, and that's why they stay away. But when they get a free ticket, they suddenly show up! So what's the truth?

As often is the case, the devil is in the details. When deciding whether or not to go to a conference, carefully check out the speakers, the agenda, and the topics. No conference will be better than its shiny brochure or a landing page—potentially only worse. On the other hand, when you go there, your experience is largely up to you. So if you want to learn something, show up on time and pay attention. If you are there to meet people, get organized and set up your meetings in advance. Brella is a fantastic tool to do that, for example.

I believe, going forward, event organizers will always say they will go ahead offline or online, as an equivalent of summer parties going ahead rain or shine. Even better, why not save on travel time and costs? Of course it's not the same, but with more online event organizing tools out there, more people will hopefully get used to it, and the experience will improve. Hopefully, people will also be as committed to attending online events as they were when they booked that trip to London or Berlin. We shall see.

Here are some highlights of the events I hosted as part of the Voice of FinTech Live Speaker Series.

Soundbite: AI—Augmented Intelligence or the Rise of the Robots?
The first Voice of FinTech Live Speaker Series event in Zurich was a lively discussion with Dorian Selz, CEO and co-founder of Squirro, an award-winning Swiss AI scale-up. Squirro provides augmented intelligence solutions to transform enterprise data into AI-driven insights for clients like Investec Asset Management, Swiss Re, ING, Natixis, and many others.

We discussed whether AI would augment our abilities so we become a better version of ourselves or if we should fear being replaced by robots powered by AI. In the debate with the guests at Sevenfriday Space in Zurich, Dorian explained without beating around the bush, "We are simply talking about machine learning; general artificial intelligence that we see in the Hollywood movies is nowhere near our generation."

Dorian added that we should focus on what we can do with the current technology and improve but not fear AI. There will be many areas where human input will still be needed, albeit the AI "revolution" may mean great changes in industries, society, and jobs.

At the event, we also had Freddy Sax, a well-known saxophone player, and DJ Candela to entertain.

Soundbite: Recruitment—Algorithms or Networking?

In another edition of the Voice of FinTech Live Speaker Series in Zurich, we enjoyed a discussion with Claudia Bolliger-Winkler, CEO and co-founder of Lionstep, an AI-powered recruitment firm.

We talked about how to find the best candidates for your company, cost-effectively. Also, as a candidate, can one beat algorithms through networking? We also spoke about the role of AI and humans in recruitment and the outlook for the balance between the two. Similar to the discussion with Squirro, the conclusion seems to be that while Lionstep is leveraging AI to execute repetitive, boring, low value-added tasks cost-efficiently, to be effective, it also leverages the technology to augment its trained staff's knowledge to deliver recruitment services to their corporate clients faster and in a more targeted manner than others, delivering better results.

At the event, we also had a bespoke selection of the outstanding modern art of Susanne di Martino, together with her model daughter Stefanja and music mixed by DJ Candela.

Digitalization of the Art Business, by Voice of FinTech: Live Speaker Series

To give you more flavor about what it's like to go to our Live Speaker Series, here is a more detailed example of what we talked about at one of our live events. We caught up with Tanya Koenig, host of "Out & About" and digital producer at CNNMoney Switzerland, after the Digitalization of the Art Business discussion as part of the Voice of FinTech Live Speaker Series in Zurich.

We were then entertained by Sina Anastasia, a rising star of the German pop scene, and enjoyed the tapas and wine from Sevenfriday Space, as always.

In this bonus podcast episode, we talked about why traditional mega art dealers invested in digital platforms, how blockchain can be useful for art buyers, and CNNMoney Switzerland's plans for increased coverage of the start-up scene. Here is the transcript of this episode:

Rudolf Falat (RF): We just wanted to talk about a couple of key themes that we discussed here live. One of them is about digital platforms for the fine arts—in other words, paintings—and my question for Tanya was I read that big mega-dealers like Gagosian invested in Artsy. Why did they invest in digital platforms? Aren't they worried about disruption, or is there another angle that you think makes sense for them?

Tanya Koenig (TK): These platforms will disrupt the art market. Then, as a big mega dealer, you'd rather be there from the start and be part of that disruption than not because you're saving your business as well, and also you'll see a shift from, of course, these older, traditional collectors that might still come to the gallery. It's all based on personal connections, but you also want to tap into new markets. These younger audiences, younger consumers, grew up with Instagram on their phones with all the information in the palm of their hands, so you want to tap into these markets too.

RF: Right. So it's basically about tapping into the new generation of the buyers, right? Getting there early, and then hopefully they grow with you, and they become your big client anyway.

TK: And also most of the art pieces that are sold are sold for less than five thousand US dollars, so in that market, probably the potential to sell an art piece through digital platform is bigger than for a million-dollar artwork.

RF: Okay, understood. Of course, we are in Switzerland, and we are at Sevenfriday Space, which is below the Trust Square, which is a well-known hub for blockchain start-ups. So we also talked about the use cases for blockchain in the art business, and one of them has to do with the provenance. Do you think that blockchain can sort out the problem of whether I'm dealing with a fake or original painting?

TK: I think blockchain certainly offers a solution to that problem because if you sell an art piece, you always need to make sure that you have the right to sell it, that it is authentic, and that you know the history or you have the provenance. For instance, in an auction, you want to know whom it belonged to before also, because this might increase the value or not so, and, often, this information is very difficult to obtain because it has not been noted down, or often the information for these artworks is difficult to obtain. Especially if an art piece has been there for a long time, how do you obtain this data? So then experts come in, and they discuss, and they might not find an agreement. You, as a buyer, have to go with an expert, or an auction house has to go with the expert that it trusts the most, so having the blockchain and starting tracking the data from the beginning, that certainly can help. The other question is, will it be used? Because obviously there are players that might also profit from the lack of information; they make a business out of it, that it's secretive. They might not have an interest in that everything is so transparent. But how can it help?

I mean, the solution is that, for instance, if there is a blockchain database, an artist, if he does a piece of art, he can put his data in there, and from there, every time it's being sold, the data is recorded, and, like that, you have a whole chain.

RF: Okay, and I guess the question is also can you use it for the old stock (or the paintings that exist) or only, you know, going forward?

TK: Going back and also the question of authenticity . . . One person in the room raised during the Live Series, he raised the problem that if you have a certificate that this art piece is a true one, you need to mark that art piece—you need to put the watermark or put the sticker on it—so that you know that is the original, or, I mean, you can still exchange with the fake, right?

RF: I think once it's on blockchain, until we have quantum computers, I guess it's safe, but what about the first entry point and connectivity to the offline world, right?

TK: It's probably a good technology going forward, yeah.

RF: You've been covering entertainment business for a while, and also I know that CNNMoney Switzerland did its Founder Series, video interviews, last summer, and I think you're going to do more of that, right?

TK: Yes, absolutely. Last year, actually, I suggested that we should do more start-up stories because it covers many things that we want to cover on CNNMoney Switzerland. So it covers business but also innovation, and usually also the entrepreneurs are interesting people to talk to, and you also get a younger audience. So we want to try to get that, so we decided that we'll focus more on start-ups. At the WEF, I covered the pre-launch of the Start-up Guide Switzerland, which is the first one portraying a lot of start-ups that are within the field of SDG and trying to do good. So I covered this pre-launch and will be doing more going forward.

RF: I saw that you spoke to Tillmann from Yova, an impact investing company that I interviewed as well on the podcast, and also last summer, I think Sandra Tobler as well, and many others.

TK: We used to do a lot of sit-down interviews; we'll do more short packages, so I think that's where you can feed in a podcast, which can go a bit more into depth and take the time to listen to people. I think it's a different usage.

RF: Different way of communicating. Yes. So thank you, Tanya, for joining us at this live event of the Voice of FinTech Live Speaker Series, and good luck.

TK: Thank you very much. Thanks for having me, and if you're curious to know more about CNNMoney Switzerland, then check out our feeds.

9

ADDITIONAL RESOURCES

Some books are to be tasted, others to be swallowed, and some few to be chewed and digested; that is, some books are to be read only in parts; others to be read, but not curiously; and some few are to be read wholly, and with diligence and attention.

— *Francis Bacon, The Essays*

I've always been an avid reader. I think so, anyway. But when you connect with your friends on some great reading apps like Goodreads, you may actually realize you are far less well-read than you would have thought. Maybe the reason is that some books, despite your best intentions, are simply too hard to finish.

You may want to at least taste some of the books mentioned in this section, thanks to apps like Goodreads, Blinkist, or getAbstract. Or, even better, try audiobooks to save time.

Nevertheless, I think it's invaluable to read up on certain topics on your own and take the best parts for yourself. Then you will feel much better equipped to digest presentations or pitches from others, often tainted by their experience or the hidden agenda you may not be aware of, or to challenge them. It's not about getting a PhD in the topic but about building a solid foundation so you can form your opinions intelligently.

Here are some of the books, research studies, or courses I have come across on my trip to the start-up world that I highly recommend reading.

For example, following up on the episode with Claudia Bienentreu, head of open innovation AXA Switzerland (AXAnauten), I'd like to share the following book tip with you. Many of you may know it, but if you are interested in innovation or open innovation and haven't read it yet, it's an absolute must-read: *The Innovator's Dilemma*, by Clayton Christensen. In this classic, the late Professor Christensen explains how even the most outstanding companies can do everything right and still get pushed aside when an innovation wave comes and fail, unless managers know how and when to abandon traditional business practices.

Following up on the podcast with Ralf Huber, co-founder of Apiax, an award-winning RegTech start-up from Switzerland, I recommend an excellent short overview of RegTech Europe, prepared by FinTech News Switzerland:

- http://fintechnews.ch/regtech/regtech-in-europe-regtech-3-0-solutions-and-more/28626/

We recorded the interview with Minh Q. Tran at Station F, the world's biggest start-up campus, which celebrated its second anniversary on June 27, 2019. If you would like to find out more about Station F, check out this article from Harriet Agnew of the *Financial Times*:

- https://www.ft.com/content/2b4a6fc8-9838-11e9-9573-ee5cbb98ed36

Following up on interviews with co-founders of Bambus.io (Franz Hoerhager) and Apiax (Ralf Huber), I'd like to share tips for excellent books that are an absolute must if you are thinking about starting your own company (or want to learn more about start-up lingo):

- *The Lean Start-up: How Constant Innovation Creates Radically Successful Businesses,* by Eric Ries: https://amzn.to/3bRyY6W
- *Lost and Founder: A Painfully Honest Field Guide to the Startup World,* by Rand Fishkin: https://amzn.to/2Xgy5Q6
- *Zero to One: Notes on Start-Ups, or How to Build the Future,* by Blake Masters: https://amzn.to/2AHqdzk

"If you can't tell who the sucker at the poker table is, it's you." This is from *Angel: How to Invest in Technology Startups,* by Jason Calacanis. Check out this great book on angel investing. This is a follow-up to the interview with David Sidler from Investiere: https://amzn.to/3cTZvBR.

"A study by McKinsey & Company estimated that, from 10,000 business ideas, 1,000 firms are founded, 100 receive venture capital, 20 go on to raise capital in an initial public offering of shares, and 2 become market leaders." This is a quote from *Mass Flourishing: How Grassroots Innovation Created Jobs, Challenge, and Change,* by Nobel Prize-winner Edmund Phelps. Founders, with odds like these, wouldn't you like to get a bit of help? Check it out on Amazon: https://amzn.to/3e7FxUA (as discussed in an interview with Kelvin Au, head of venture at the Founders Factory in London, about investing and entrepreneurship).

Also check out *Founder's Pocket Guide on Cap Tables* (https://amzn.to/2LONnq0) as a followup to the podcast episode with Mazin Biviji, co-founder of Toquity, a blockchain solution for cap tables.

In episode 9, we talked to one of the leading VCs in Switzerland and the DACH region, Redalpine. Founders, if you want to be well prepared when fundraising from VCs, you should get this excellent book by Brad Feld and Jason Mendelson: *Venture Deals*. It has everything you need to know when you want to raise money for your company or sell it (https://amzn.to/2LPcrgC).

In episode 10, we talked to Marwan El-Hakim, partner at Veridian Ventures, a London-based business angel syndicate. He warned founders against a temptation to push for an unrealistic valuation in the early fundraising rounds. I enjoyed the dramatization of this problem in HBO's hit comedy show "Silicon Valley" (season 2, episode 1):

> *Huh. I suppose you could argue it might have been easier to hit more realistic benchmarks and reach cashflow breakeven,"* Javeed says, realizing the magnitude of the disaster he caused himself. *"And then we wouldn't have faced that down-round. And we wouldn't have had to settle for acquisition. . . . No, no, we could have done a legit series B. I'd still be CEO. I'd have my job, my kickass house, I'd probably still have my girlfriend . . . Why didn't anyone tell me I could take less!"* (https://www.washingtonpost.com/news/act-four/wp/2015/04/17/silicon-valleys-perfect-take-on-our-tech-madness/?noredirect=on)

If you missed the show, see the official season 2 trailer on YouTube (https://youtu.be/qCj9Lm4fRQY), and I am sure you will want to watch the entire six seasons.

In the following episode, we talked to Francois Briod, CEO and co-founder of Monito, a Lausanne-based money transfer comparison site. Find out more about Lausanne as a major start-up hub in this article from Sifted:

> *How Lausanne's tech companies punch above their weight: Lausanne creates about the same number of start-ups as Zurich does, with only a third of the population. This is how the city's tech community manages to punch above its weight.* (from *Sifted, https://sifted.eu/articles/lausanne-tech-hub/*)

When we talked to Annie Guo, CEO and founder of SilkPay, I asked her where the name of her company comes from. She reminded me of the Silk Road, and I'd like to flag the book with the same name for you. Far more than just a history of the Silk Roads, this book attempts to re-center our typical view of the history of the world (https://amzn.to/2ZoyhiT).

In relation to the episode with Matthias Zwingli from digitalswitzerland, I'd like to highlight a fantastic, hands-on, online course from MIT, which I took not long ago, that can help you to upgrade your digital skills. You can see the preview of the Digital Transformation course with Dr. Abel Sanchez and Dr. John Williams on YouTube: https://youtu.be/NwwazhND9BA.

In an interview with Mona Zoet, founder of RegPac Revolution, a RegTech ecosystem builder and accelerator based in Singapore, and F10 Hackathon Singapore's local partner, Mona shared her views on the status of the FinTech and RegTech scene in Singapore in comparison to Europe. *The Future Is Asian*, writes Dr. Parag Khanna in his excellent book. At the Asia Society's event in Zurich, Parag explained that if you look at recent history objectively, Asianization of the world economy has been happening for a long time. Let's see what happens after the dust settles after the coronavirus crisis. You can find it here: https://amzn.to/2X6zzxA.

Concerning the episode on VC investing with Jatin Rajput, here is an awesome well of wisdom: "The world is undeniably flat—and the global playing field has never been more open to start-up opportunities" (from *Secrets of Sand Hill Road: Venture Capital and How to Get It*, by Scott Kupor, managing partner at Andreessen Horowitz). This book is the definitive guide bridging the information asymmetry between entrepreneurs and VCs. You can get it on Amazon at https://amzn.to/2ymJohh.

Following up on the interview with Ravina Mutha and Pranay Jain from Enterprise Bot about entrepreneurship, chatbots, NLP, and artificial intelligence, I'd like to highlight an excellent book for you that explains about how AI will impact the workplace in the future: *The Future of Leadership: Rise of Automation, Robotics and Artificial Intelligence*, by the very popular Brigette Hyacinth. You can get it on Amazon at https://amzn.to/2LLXV9p.

Following up on an interview with Tillmann Lang, CEO and co-founder of Yova, on how to invest in line with your values even if you are a retail client, I would like to highlight a great initiative supporting all UN sustainable goals, called Togetherband. Togetherband unites a global community, sharing a commitment to all of the seventeen UN sustainable development goals (ESG). It aims to bring together one billion active citizens to achieve these goals. You can wear your Togetherband as a symbol of support for the goals. Togetherbands are crafted using innovative and sustainable materials, are handmade in Nepal from upcycled ocean plastic, and the clasp is made from decommissioned illegal firearms. You can read more about why David Beckham became their ambassador in this article in *Elle* magazine: https://www.elle.com/uk/life-and-culture/a28842198/david-beckham-ambassador-togetherband/.

I, of course, got mine a while ago. My band is supporting quality education. Check it out here: https://togetherband.org/.

We talked to Sandra Tobler, co-founder and CEO of Futurae Technologies, a Zurich-based cybersecurity start-up, about the latest solutions to provide cybersecurity to corporate clients, including banks. Or should cybersecurity be a public good? In this article, WEF argues that we must treat cybersecurity as a public good: https://www.weforum.org/agenda/2019/08/we-must-treat-cybersecurity-like-public-good/.

In an interview with Pascal Allot, IBM innovation ecosystem director, we talked about what IBM offers start-ups in Switzerland to support them on their journey: software credits, Design Thinking studio, and more.

If you are thinking about changing your career, note Garry Kasparov's example. Ever since, as the first world-chess champion, he lost to the IBM DeepBlue supercomputer, he has become a renowned speaker on artificial intelligence. He gave a great keynote speech during the Machine Learning Days at Lausanne's EPFL in January 2019, with a telling title: "How Machine Learning Upgrades Human Creativity." You can learn more about AI and humans in his book *Deep Thinking* (https://amzn.to/2WRiCak).

In connection with the interview with Stefan Muehlemann, founder and CEO of Loanboox and a serial entrepreneur, about how he got started with his latest venture, I'd like to highlight the following classic by Jim Collins, *How Do You Go from Being Good to Great?* You can get this book on Amazon at https://amzn.to/2zWHIvc.

In the episode called "The Future of Money by SIX—Is Cash Dead?" we spoke with Alexander Verbeck, head of cash ecosystem at SIX, a financial service provider that operates in the infrastructure of Switzerland's financial center, about the white paper on the future of money that Alex and his team published shortly before. Here are the scenarios as published on SIX's website: https://www.six-group.com/en/company/innovation/research-reports/picture-of-the-future-money.html?utm_campaign=vanity%20url&utm_medium=redirect&utm_source=www.six-group.com%2Ffuture-money.

On the same page, you can also follow an illustrative journey of Felix to visualize the most likely scenario that digital rules can mean for our daily lives in 2025 and read the summaries or the full white paper in English and German here.

"You can't do it alone! How to find high-quality talent for your venture and what to look for"—In this interview with William Laitinen, managing director of Exige International, a UK and Swiss executive search firm specializing in recruitment for global financial services companies and FinTech, we talked about what to look for in your co-founders and what traits you should focus on when building a successful team. As a follow-up, you can also read more on the importance of judiciously selecting co-founders for your venture in this article from INSEAD Knowledge: https://knowledge.insead.edu/leadership-organisations/start-ups-the-founding-team-is-a-real-magic-bullet-13111.

"Somebody stole my unicorn! Make sure it doesn't happen to you"—In this podcast, we speak to Christian Meisser, the CEO of LEXR, a Zurich-based legal services company that focuses on tech, FinTech, and digital businesses. I highly recommend taking a very relevant course I took last year from the Start-Up Board Academy, which focuses on the Start-Up Board's obligations and dynamics. Check it out here and book early—it's often sold out months in advance: https://www.startupboardacademy.ch/.

"INSEAD in Davos"—In this bonus episode, we caught up with Peter Zemsky, deputy dean of INSEAD and dean of innovation, after an INSEAD-hosted panel on artificial intelligence, "Balancing AI productivity and responsibility," in the SDG tent in Davos during WEF 2020. Tanya König from CNNMoney Switzerland, and a guest at our live event in February, explains the WEF's history in this short video on YouTube: https://youtu.be/tLK82vssGbE.

In the interview with Anders Christensen, who is the head of ecosystem at Avaloq.one in Zurich, Switzerland, we talked about how Avaloq has been increasing its commitment to open innovation and partnerships through start-ups by establishing Avaloq.one's platform. If you are interested in how to grow your venture and feel like you can benefit from comprehensive financial knowledge tailored specifically to start-ups, here is an outstanding book I read recently, *Entrepreneurial Finance* (https://amzn.to/3ecPdND.)

In the episode on R3 ("Enterprise blockchain solutions for corporates and start-ups"), we talk to Yves Guillaume A. Messy about what enterprise blockchain means, its relevance to financial services, and R3's cooperation with F10. A great complement to this is the TED Talk from Don Tapscott explaining blockchain on YouTube (https://youtu.be/Pl8OlkkwRpc) in his legendary book, *Blockchain Revolution* (https://amzn.to/2TqBgnb). I highly recommend reading it; whether you're a fan or a critic, it's best to form your own view.

With Ghassen Benhadjsalah, a serial entrepreneur based in Switzerland, we talked about direct lending (or P2P lending) in general. Then we focused on Swiss SMEs, why this market is an excellent opportunity for both SMEs needing financing and lenders/investors, and how it all works, as well as Acredius's competitive edge over other platforms or banks. One of the key messages from this interview is the ever-important need to diversify. Just like Sir Templeton said, "The only investors who shouldn't diversify are those who are right 100% of the time."

Learn more about the John Templeton Foundation, its funding areas, and grants it provides here: https://www.templeton.org/.

In the Danube Valley podcast, we talk to Matej Ftacnik, cofounder of Vacuumlabs, based in Bratislava, Slovakia. Vacuum Labs is a FinTech-focused software engineering powerhouse with over two hundred employees, taking innovations to the markets around the world, building neobanks for incumbents in Asia, for example, and building the back end and front end from scratch for the twenty-first century. Find out more about how they think in their article on "The Mysterious World of Core Banking" (https://inside.vacuumlabs.com/fintech/the-mysterious-world-of-core-banking).

In connection with the short interviews with Paris FinTech Forum, I would like to share some additional resources, several of which are authored or co-authored by the guests on the podcast:

- Clara Durodie, chair of Cognitive Finance Group, London, about artificial intelligence for financial services: You can get the book *Decoding AI in Financial Services* directly from the Cognitive Finance Group website: https://www.cognitivefinance.ai/product-page/DecodingAI.
- Ian O'Sullivan, European lead of Mastercard Start Path: Check out the research report "FinTech in 2020: Five Global Trends to Watch" (https://newsroom.mastercard.com/wp-content/uploads/2020/01/Start-Path-_-CB-Insights-2020-Trends-Report_FINAL.pdf).
- Susanne Chishti, CEO of FinTech Circle and FinTech Circle Institute: Check out their latest book, *PayTech*, on Amazon: https://amzn.to/2LOPSIU

- Emmalyn Shaw, managing partner of Flourish Ventures, San Francisco: Check out the blog of Flourish Ventures here: https://flourishventures.com/perspectives/forbes-the-forbes-fintech-50-the-most-innovative-fintech-companies-in-2020/.

"Founder story: Who is the best research analyst? Invisage has the answer"—We talked about how to objectively evaluate research analysts using model portfolios. In this time of market turmoil, what's the book you wish you had read a long time ago? I'd say *The Black Swan*. Get it on Amazon: https://amzn.to/3gcjQUT.

In the middle of lockdowns being implemented in Europe, we released the episode "Financial markets technology: VC perspective." I thought it would be interesting to see some of the early thoughts on the impact of the health crisis on start-ups by renowned VC investors like Sequoia Capital. See the article called "Coronavirus: The Black Swan of 2020" here: https://medium.com/sequoia-capital/coronavirus-the-black-swan-of-2020-7c72bdeb9753.

"Finovate Berlin"—In the interview with Myles Stephenson, CEO of Modulr, we talked about the Copernican leap in banking in the UK. Find out more by going back to the original, legendary deck on the Copernican Revolution in banking, by F. Rotman from QED Investors: https://drive.google.com/viewerng/viewer?url=https://fintechjunkie.files.wordpress.com/2018/04/the-copernican-revolution-in-banking.pdf.

In the episode called "Wealth management versus WealthTech," we talk to Christine (Mar) Ciriani about wealth management challenges and where WealthTech companies could provide solutions and add value for high net worth or ultra-high net worth clients. If you would like to gain a comprehensive overview of WealthTech, check out the *WealthTech* book by the FinTech Circle: https://fintechcircle.com/wealthtech-book/.

"Founder story: In vino veritas—How to invest in the wine businesses"—Here we talk to Maxime Debure, INSEAD alumnus, former winemaker, and management consultant, about investing in wine versus investing in wine estates, either through crowdfunding or private equity type of deals. If you would like to buy outstanding fine wine online, don't go any further. These are recommended by Maxime:

- Les Grappes is a marketplace offering to buy directly from a wide selection of one thousand wine growers. The wine is shipped directly from the estate to your door in France and neighboring countries. Promo code GOWINEMAKERS will give you a €15 discount for €100 spent. See www.lesgrappes.com.
- LBV stands for Le Bon Vin, which offers a selection of wines shortlisted by a jury of professionals and fine connoisseurs. Promo code FINTECH10 will give you a €25 discount for €250 spent. Go to www.lbvselection.com.
- Palate Club is "AI for wine": AI is used to understand your taste to deliver wine to your door that your palate will enjoy. Promo code FINTECH10 will give you a $10 discount on any purchase. Only available in the US. Visit www.palateclub.com.

In the episode "Core banking in the cloud with Thought Machine," we talk to Paul Taylor, CEO and founder of Thought Machine, a London-headquartered cloud-native core banking technology company, about why running your infrastructure in the cloud is the way to go. See more in this blog post by Paul Taylor, CEO of Thought Machine: "CEO Views: Why are cloud systems so much more reliable?" (https://www.thoughtmachine.net/blog/ceo-views-why-are-cloud-systems-so-much-more-reliable).

"A migration to the cloud is a golden opportunity to abandon unstable legacy systems from a by-gone era and shift to rock-solid applications, written from scratch on Cloud Native principles" (Paul Taylor, Thought Machine).

"The InsurTech Series: The government and the start-ups, with A. Silberschmidt"—In this episode, we speak to Andri Silberschmidt, entrepreneur and the youngest member of the Swiss Parliament, about his entrepreneurial journey, what drew him to politics, his views on Switzerland as a home for start-ups, the Swiss government's measures to help start-ups deal with the COVID-19 pandemic, and his early thoughts on the world after lockdown. See the summary of the support measures for start-ups in Switzerland, prepared by FinTech News Switzerland, here: https://fintechnews.ch/covid19/covid-19-support-innovative-swiss-startups-to-receive-federal-funding-support/34673/. These include short-term work support packages and loans.

An excellent overview of the support measures in France, the United Kingdom, Germany, Italy, Spain, Ireland, Portugal, the Nordics, and others was prepared by Sifted: https://sifted.eu/articles/coronavirus-support-startups/.

"Design Thinking with IBM and fundraising with the Voice of FinTech"—It all begins with an idea. Maybe you want to launch a business. Maybe you want to turn a hobby into something more. Or perhaps you have a project to share with the world. In today's world, you'd better be prepared. In April 2020, we held a webinar with IBM on "Design Thinking and Fundraising." Check out my presentation on how to avoid major pitfalls when raising funds for the first time: https://www.slideshare.net/RudolfFalat/fundraising-for-earlystage-startups.

In addition, here is a short video about IBM's approach to Design Thinking: https://youtu.be/jU4fTt2DszE. You should also have a look at the resources for start-ups provided by IBM:

https://developer.ibm.com/startups/, https://www.ibm.com/design/thinking/.

Emerging technology due diligence—how? In this interview with Rodney Reis, co-founder and CEO of Avalia Systems from Switzerland, we talked about conducting due diligence on emerging technologies. Please see a highly relevant further reading here: https://www.prnewswire.com/news-releases/emerging-technology-innovation-assessment-tool-available-from-comptia-301009267.html.

Following up on the interview with Shruti Van Dyke Gandhi from Array Ventures in San Francisco, don't miss out on the blog post from Jason Calacanis on whether now it's the right time to be an angel investor: https://calacanis.com/2020/03/27/now-is-the-best-time-to-be-an-angel-investor-let-me-show-you-how/.

In relation to the interview with Sven Siat from SIX on open banking from the Financial Markets Series, I recommend also checking out the interview with Cornelius Dorn, Head Strategy and Business Development, Banking Services at SIX: https://www.six-group.com/en/blog/2019/open-banking-standards.html.

Following up on an interview with Marc Gruber from EPFL, apart from his book, *Where to Play* (you can find it here: https://amzn.to/2WRC9qW), check out also Steve Blank's blog post about the Market Opportunity Navigator described in the book here: https://steveblank.com/2019/05/07/how-to-stop-playing-target-market-roulette-a-new-addition-to-the-lean-toolset/.

In an interview with Ute Koenig-Stemmler from VISA, we talked about VISA's start-up program. You can find out more here: https://usa.visa.com/visa-everywhere/everywhere-initiative/initiative-europe.html.

You can also watch an interview with Janine Haendel, CEO of Roger Federer Foundation on CNNMoney Switzerland: https://youtu.be/gRKn-bxLv1I.

Brett King has written several insightful books on banking and FinTech, from *Breaking Banks* to *Bank 2.0, Bank 3.0, Bank 4.0*, and others. Find out more about his book, podcast, radio show and speaking engagements on his website http://brettking.com/. As mentioned, he also has an inspiring book coming out later this year, which you can pre-order on Amazon, called *The Rise of Technosocialism*: https://amzn.to/2LUtjT6, about the future of humans as species. Check it out and let me know what you think about it at info@voiceoffintech.com. Check out also Breaking banks episode where Sci-Fi legends talk COVID-19 here: https://provoke.fm/sci-fi-legends-talk-covid-19/.

As you can see from the above list, there are many resources out there that you can use to navigate on your trip to the start-up world. This doesn't have to be a trial and error experience where you get lost half of the time. Let's leverage the wisdom of others to improve the odds of survival and ultimately the success on your mission, whether you are an innovator, investor, start-up founder or FinTech or start-up enthusiast.

10

CONCLUSION

In this book, I have tried to glue together what I've learned from doing the Voice of FinTech podcast, networking, participating at start-up events, conducting research, and reading on topics such as entrepreneurship, leadership, investing, and the various flavors of FinTech. Here are some key takeaways:

Incumbents. When it comes to incumbents and the start-up cooperation discussion, I hope people can be honest with each other and share early on what their objectives are and what is feasible and what is not. Start-ups don't have time for months or years of working on a highly customized proof of concept; they need to productize it and sell it to others. It is also tempting for consultants to use start-ups as a cheap way of backfilling certain roles, especially with an IT background, but I do hope they will shy away from that. Building something great together should be the objective.

Investors. The competition is getting more and more fierce, so relying solely on inbound leads from their network will not cut it. Remember, great ideas can come from anywhere, as Geoff Ralston said on the Voice of FinTech. So give everyone with a cool idea a chance, whether they are your friends of friends or not.

Start-up founders. Learn about entrepreneurial finance. What you do is incredibly hard, so why not take a little bit of time to improve your chances? A big part of that is a commitment to diversity; it will undoubtedly help your odds to have people who look and sound different from you and, most importantly, think differently from you.

Incubators, accelerators, or hubs. Obviously, every start-up trying to get to some of these programs should do its due diligence and see if there is a fit between start-up objectives and what such programs can offer. In my view, a first-time founder can definitely benefit from such programs, no doubt.

Thought leaders and events. Well, we have seen a great deal of disruption around the world recently, and many industries have been hit hard. The event industry is certainly one of them. I still believe that there is a future for conferences and meet-ups around the world, although we may have to approach them differently. I am certainly looking forward to catching up with many thought leaders and influencers in the FinTech space or start-up world very soon.

I hope you found this book useful. If you have any feedback regarding the book or the Voice of FinTech podcast, please contact me at info@voiceoffintech.com. I'd be happy to hear from you.

Sincerely,
Rudolf Falat
P.S. Check out https://www.voiceoffintech.com/ for all podcasts.

ABOUT THE AUTHOR

The Voice of FinTech podcast was founded by Rudolf Falat, senior corporate finance professional with extensive experience in financial services, based in Zurich, Switzerland, in June 2019. Rudolf is a FinTech and tech enthusiast, start-up mentor, advisor, business angel, and executive education coach.

The Voice of FinTech is a weekly podcast interview with FinTech founders and key players in the FinTech ecosystem in Switzerland and Europe. It is both educational and inspirational.

Looking to see how others have made it? How to avoid their mistakes? Who can help you in terms of advice, funding, or opening doors? Which are the best start-ups to invest in or partner up with? The Voice of FinTech is here for you.

You can hear some of the views on themes appearing in this podcast when Pete Townsend interviewed Rudolf on his Money Never Sleeps podcast.

This book is a collection of Voice of FinTech podcast highlights and additional resources, explained and connected together by the author.

See more at www.rudolffalat.com.

REFERENCES

Voice of FinTech podcast episodes in chronological order:

1. F10—Home of FinTech
2. AXAnauten—Open innovation with AXA
3. Apiax—RegTech founder story
4. Odysseus Partners—Asset builder
5. Bambus—DACH FinTech founder story
6. Investiere—Investment platform for start-ups in Switzerland
7. Founders Factory—Global partner for start-ups and scale-ups
8. Toquity—Cap Table Solution for founders and investors by INSEAD alumni
9. Redalpine—European technology and health tech VC
10. Veridian Ventures—Business angel syndicate
11. Monito—Founder story: Stop overpaying when sending money abroad!
12. Silkpay—Founder story: Chinese mobile payment acceptance solutions (Alipay and WeChat Pay) for European merchants
13. digitalswitzerland—Platform to drive digital transformation across the country

14. RegPac Revolution and F10 Hackathon Singapore
15. Union Park Ventures: From a banker to a VC investor
16. Soundbite: *The Future Is Asian*, by Dr. Parag Khanna
17. Soundbite: AI—Augmented Intelligence or the Rise of the Robots? with Squirro
18. Enterprise Bot—Founders story: Customer service that works!
19. Yova—Founder story: Make the world a better place and make money at the same time!
20. Futurae Technologies—Founder story: When a dog is not enough to protect your assets!
21. IBM Innovation Ecosystem—Start-up with IBM
22. Singularity Group—Investing in exponential progress and innovation
23. Soundbite: SwissCognitive—The Global AI Hub and We Shape Tech
24. Loanboox—Founder story: Making raising big-ticket debt painless
25. Swiss Finance Start-ups and Swiss FinTech Fair—Keen Innovation, Tradeplus24, and FinTech News
26. Soundbite with Geoff Ralston: Y Combinator visiting Europe
27. Innovation at Generali
28. Soundbite: Recruitment—Algorithms or networking? Lionstep
29. SEBA— A bank for digital assets
30. F10 goes to Singapore!
31. Seedstars World—Emerging markets start-up ecosystem builders!
32. Soundbite with Eric Sarasin, chairman of Singularity Group
33. Check6Wealth—How to make reporting easy and exciting again!
34. TEDx Zurich: The Power of 10

35. Xoogler.co—Start-up community of Googlers and Google alumni
36. Soph.IA summit—Innovation and start-ups at the French Riviera Sophia Club and SAP
37. Swiss FinTech Investor Day: SICTIC, Unconventional Ventures, and eQTiq
38. Voice of FinTech meets Global Tech Box! An ultimate podcast and vlog crossover
39. Future of money by SIX—Is cash dead?
40. You can't do it alone! How to find high-quality talent for your venture and what to look for
41. Somebody stole my unicorn! How to make sure it doesn't happen to you . . . with LEXR
42. INSEAD in Davos!
43. Avaloq.one—A new marketplace for B2B FinTechs
44. R3—Enterprise blockchain solutions for corporates and start-ups!
45. Digitalization of the art business with Tanya Koenig from CNNMoney Switzerland
46. Direct lending for SMEs in Switzerland with Acredius
47. The Danube Valley: Vacuum Labs example
48. Paris FinTech Forum: Cognitive Finance Group, Mastercard, FinTech Circle, and Flourish Ventures
49. MassChallenge Lausanne: A million francs for you?
50. Terra Ventures: A sneak peek into the Israeli VC mindset
51. Founder story: Who is the best research analyst? Invisage has the answer
52. Financial Markets Technology: VC perspective
53. Swiss FinTech Awards 2020—And the winners are . . .
54. Finovate Berlin

55. Founder story: Last mile in data analytics with Luminant Analytics
56. Wealth management versus WealthTech
57. Founder story: Pivoting to scale with Rapyd and guest co-host Adelle Grisaffe from RFi Group's Global Digital Banker podcast
58. Founder story: In vino veritas—How to invest in wine businesses
59. Core banking in the cloud with Thought Machine
60. The InsurTech Series: The government and the start-ups with Andri Silberschmidt
61. Emerging Technology Due Diligence—How?
62. Investing in Enterprise Technology and Scaling Up: A Bay Area VC Perspective
63. The Financial Markets Series: Open Banking in Switzerland
64. The InsurTech Series: Where to Play with Marc Gruber, VP Innovation EPFL, Lausanne
65. Open Innovation in Central Europe with VISA
66. Discussion with Janine Haendel, CEO of Roger Federer Foundation
67. One Year Anniversary Special: Breaking Banks with Brett King

www.ingramcontent.com/pod-product-compliance
Lightning Source LLC
Chambersburg PA
CBHW050244220526
45465CB00002B/540